PLAYING THE VICTIM

ALSO BY KYLIE CHEUNG

Coercion (Pluto Press)

Survivor Injustice (North Atlantic Books)

A Woman's Place (North Atlantic Books)

The Gaslit Diaries (Thought Catalog Books)

My Boyfriend the Superhero (AK Press)

PLAYING THE VICTIM

HOW THE POWERFUL DENY AND ATTACK SURVIVORS OF VIOLENCE, FROM DOMESTIC ABUSE TO GENOCIDE

KYLIE CHEUNG

North Atlantic Books
Huichin, unceded Ohlone land
Berkeley, California

North Atlantic Books
An educational nonprofit organization
Huichin, unceded Ohlone land
2526 Martin Luther King Jr Way
Berkeley, CA 94704 USA
www.northatlanticbooks.com

Cover design by Jess Morphew
Book design by Happenstance Type-O-Rama

Acquisitions editor: Shayna Keyles • Production editor: Erin Wiegand
Copyeditor: Adrienne Armstrong • Proofreader: Justine Hart
Indexer: Reed Floarea

North Atlantic Books's publications are distributed to the US trade and internationally by Penguin Random House Publisher Services. For further information, visit our website at www.northatlanticbooks.com.

The authorized representative in the EU for product safety and compliance is Eucomply OÜ, Pärnu mnt 139b-14, 11317 Tallinn, Estonia, hello@eucompliancepartner.com, +33757690241.

Library of Congress Cataloging-in-Publication Data

Names: Cheung, Kylie– author
Title: Playing the victim : how the powerful deny and attack survivors of violence, from domestic abuse to genocide/Kylie Cheung.
Description: Berkeley, CA : North Atlantic Books, [2026] | Includes bibliographical references and index. | Summary: "Playing the Victim offers critical analysis into how imperialist powers and capitalist institutions have co-opted the tactics of domestic abusers to maintain brutal regimes of oppression—particularly, the tactic of DARVO (deny, attack, reverse victim-offender)—as they justify their violence and crush dissent. Those most harmed are often, themselves, victims of varying forms of domestic abuse"— Provided by publisher.
Identifiers: LCCN 2026001315 (print) | LCCN 2026001316 (ebook) | ISBN 9798889844020 trade paperback | ISBN 9798889844037 ebook
Subjects: LCSH: Imperialism | Power (Social sciences) | Blaming the victim—Political aspects | Victims of crimes | Women—Violence against
Classification: LCC JC359 .C477 2026 (print) | LCC JC359 (ebook)
LC record available at https://lccn.loc.gov/2026001315
LC ebook record available at https://lccn.loc.gov/2026001316

The interior of this book is printed on 100 percent recycled paper, and the cover is printed on material from well-managed forests.

1 2 3 4 5 6 7 8 9 MARQUIS 31 30 29 28 27 26

Printed in Canada

CONTENTS

INTRODUCTION

In the spring of 2022, I reported extensively on a celebrity trial that I initially wanted to see as just that: a celebrity trial. Instead, *Depp v. Heard* would fundamentally alter my understanding of power, patriarchy, and even empire. Johnny Depp, a man repeatedly accused of physical violence and volatile, drunken behavior spanning decades, sued his ex-wife Amber Heard over a 2018 op-ed in which Heard recounted surviving an abusive relationship without so much as naming Depp. It should have been obvious that Heard, more than twenty years Depp's junior and armed with extensive, horrific evidence of years of physical abuse perpetrated by Depp, was the victim. Instead, Depp's legal team and the general public wielded mere evidence of her resistance and reactions to Depp's abuse to frame *Heard* as the abuser and *Depp* as her victim. Heard was forced to pay Depp millions in damages. She was all but driven from the country with her young daughter as a result of a breathtakingly vitriolic hate campaign, which saw brands, celebrities, and entire social platforms train their misogynistic ire on her.

Depp v. Heard was singularly horrifying in its influence and reach. The trial was followed by a reported spike in abusers suing their victims in retaliation for speaking out about their abuse. But the trial was, at its core, a large-scale example of an everyday reality. That reality is DARVO, a strategy often weaponized by domestic abusers, which stands for *deny, attack, reverse victim and offender*.[1]

Psychologist Jennifer Freyd introduced the concept of DARVO in 1997—a culmination of years of research into the psychology of abusive dynamics and the tactics of abusers when their behaviors are challenged. In the journal *Feminism & Psychology*, Freyd wrote,

"I have observed that actual abusers threaten, bully and make a nightmare for anyone who holds them accountable or asks them to change their abusive behavior. This attack, intended to chill and terrify, typically includes threats of lawsuits, overt and covert attacks on the whistle-blower's credibility, and so on." DARVO relies heavily on character assassination, often fundamentally misogynistic in nature, "ridiculing the person who attempts to hold the offender accountable." The abuser "rapidly creates the impression" that *they* are "the wronged one, while the victim or concerned observer is the offender. . . . The offender is on the offense and the person attempting to hold the offender accountable is put on the defense."

In an article published nearly three decades later, in 2024, Freyd and fellow researchers note that perpetrators of abuse wielded DARVO tactics in 72 percent of cases involving interpersonal violence among undergraduate students.[2] DARVO lies at the crux of reactionary movements that have sprung up in the years since MeToo—a movement that exposed the pervasive, universal nature of gender-based violations in society, entering the mainstream in 2017. These reactionary movements include HimToo, which attempts to frame "false accusations" as far more prevalent than they are in reality. President Donald Trump famously said in 2018, "It's a very scary time for young men in America,"[3] after then–Supreme Court Justice nominee Brett Kavanaugh faced several sexual misconduct allegations.

According to a 2021 survey by Know Your IX, a survivor justice legal advocacy organization, 23 percent of student survivors said their perpetrator threatened to sue them for defamation, 19 percent said they were warned by their school of the possibility of defamation suits, and 10 percent have faced "retaliatory complaints" filed by their assailants.[4] One Know Your IX organizer at the time told me that, like Heard, most student survivors weren't subjected to defamation lawsuits or threats because they publicly named their abuser, but simply because they told their friends and campus communities they had been assaulted. That alone—seeking support—was an act of abuse, according to the warped, patriarchal logic of the American legal system and the institutions that reproduce it.

The Depp–Heard trial and all its revelations stayed with me—especially as other public figures accused of abuse continued to wield the same playbook. A year later, actor Jonathan Majors's legal team claimed his ex-girlfriend Grace Jabbari, who he'd left with several visible injuries, had abused *him*, pointing to her acts of self-defense.[5] This—characterizing Jabbari as the one who was dangerous to Majors—is "how DARVO works," sexual violence researcher Dr. Nicole Bedera told me in 2023. She explained, "It's about bringing up things the victim has done to suggest the victim is not a perfect victim, they're not a deserving victim, they're not a good victim. Sometimes they deny the abuse happened, and sometimes they just deny that it was wrong, because it was actually 'self-defense.'"

Beyond popular culture, DARVO intensely shaped my political analysis too, as I watched anti-abortion activists continually claim they had no choice but to light abortion clinics on fire and implicitly or explicitly threaten the lives of abortion providers, all in defense of "unborn babies," they said. In a similar vein, the 2020s have been defined by sharply exacerbated transphobia and xenophobia in American politics and the West writ large, by cruel and dehumanizing laws and political movements to terrorize the most vulnerable among us—all justified by presenting those with the least power as the oppressors in our society.

But never have I been more struck by the overtness of DARVO in the realm of political theater than in 2023, as Israel launched the latest, appallingly devastating iteration of its decades-long genocide against Palestinians, an extermination campaign against a captive population largely comprising children. None of this would have been possible without a bottomless fount of funding and weapons by the United States and the West. The gruesome details of this genocide are devastating. But these details make up the lived reality of Palestinians in Gaza, and we can't—and won't—look away from them in this book.

On October 7, 2023, the Gaza-based political group Hamas launched an offensive on Israeli settlers, many of whom were soldiers in Israel's army, which leads the world in the systematic murder of children. Soon thereafter, Israel used this attack as a pretext to drop the equivalent of several nuclear bombs on Gaza within days of October 7. Tens of thousands of disproportionately Palestinian women and children were killed in a matter of weeks. Israel bombed tents, refugee camps, hospital after hospital after hospital.[6] For years, long before October 7, Israel ensured that Gaza led the world in child amputees per capita.[7] Nonetheless, through every act of barbarism, the justification—by Israel and the Western politicians who function as its proxies—remained the same: "Israel has a right to defend itself."

Sometimes they deny the abuse happened, and sometimes they just deny that it was wrong, because it was actually "self-defense."

Since 2023, there has been a groundswell of support for Palestine across the United States. Pollsters have called the massive shift in public beliefs about Israel and Palestine a "sea change." Zionist critics have tried to mock this shift, referring to widespread support for Palestine and the centering of the issue within progressive and leftist organizing as a trendy "omnicause," accusing pro-Palestine activists of forcing the issue down the public's throat. But in many ways, they're precisely right: Palestine *is* an omnicause.

A genocide should matter to citizens of the world regardless of its direct impacts on our own lives. But on top of that, the genocide in Gaza and Israel's ability to enact a modern Holocaust with both impunity and unending US support is inseparable from our national political realities and American body politic. Gaza and Palestine writ large have become a laboratory for Israel and the United States to test a range of barbaric weapons and surveillance systems.[8] And Gaza has become a site for endless brutality toward pregnant women in a genocidal attempt to wipe an entire ethnic group off the map—the ultimate form of reproductive violence, at a time when we're witnessing our own reproductive rights systematically dismantled in the United States. The second Trump administration quickly set to work unleashing a shocking crusade against free speech, pressuring and controlling media companies, repressing student organizing, effectively declaring war on universities. Years of state attacks on pro-Palestine speech helped pave the way for this repression. Israel's brutal, supremacist campaigns have become the ultimate test of what an ethnostate can get away with on the world stage—all by couching their actions in the language of victimhood.

And, most pertinent to my research and the arguments I put forward in my writing about gender-based violence, the genocide against Palestinians, and the frameworks through which Israel and the US war machine have justified this genocide, model *exactly* how imperialist oppressors wield DARVO to terrorize with impunity.

DARVO isn't just a framework to understand interpersonal violence. It's also a framework to understand state violence, fascist political movements, imperialist warfare, colonial occupation, the full range of state-sanctioned attacks on our bodies and lives. When you peel back the layers, you find the language and strategies of DARVO everywhere.

Israel–Palestine presents an especially salient case study.

Slogans of liberation and resistance, like "free Palestine," "from the river to the sea, Palestine will be free," or "globalize the Intifada," are framed by Zionists as a call for genocide against all Jewish people and the death and extermination of all Israelis—even as, in our non-hypothetical reality, this is precisely what Israel's very existence has resulted in for Palestinians. These aforementioned slogans are calls for freedom, for a right to live, to move, to be human; but even if they were incitements of violence, they would still be words, wishes, demands. Why are we to believe those words are more threatening, more dangerous, more genocidal than the actual genocide that

Israel is perpetrating? Why are we to accept the premise that wishing for freedom—by those without power, by the colonized and oppressed—is wishing for genocide? If there is such a thing as a genocidal slogan, is it not "Israel has a right to defend itself"? These words, as we have seen for decades now, precede and justify an endless onslaught of death, destruction, and actual genocide. If there is such a thing as a genocidal slogan, it's "Israel has a right to defend itself" or "Israel has a right to exist."

I first learned about the oppression of Palestinians under Israel's regime of apartheid, terror, and displacement through my campus anti-rape activism in college. Sexual violence against Palestinians was and is indelibly baked into Israel's occupation of Palestine. To so much as move from one place to another across occupied Palestine requires passage through invasive checkpoints operated by the Israeli army; many of these checkpoints require crude body searches that amount to daily sexual assaults and other indignities.[9] One human rights advocate at the Women's Centre for Legal Aid and Counselling (WCLAC) told me in 2025 about cases of parents so desperate to protect their children from this routine sexual abuse that they would feel compelled to marry off their daughters at young ages, so they could escape the Israeli occupation and live safely elsewhere. There was no other way out of such routine sexual degradation.

Since the events of October 7, the WCLAC advocate told me that the organization observed an increase in reported incidents of sexual violence against dozens of Palestinian women and girls in the West Bank, Gaza, and Jerusalem. According to the organization, the experiences of Palestinian women detained by Israeli authorities share the same elements: Women are systematically arrested without charges and held under administrative detention. They recount being searched, forced to strip, repeatedly beaten on their genitals, photographed naked, and threatened with or sometimes subjected to rape.

In March 2025, the United Nations Independent International Commission of Inquiry on the Occupied Palestinian Territory published a report focused on gender-based violations committed by Israel, including rape, sexual torture, and targeted attacks on Palestinian women's ability to safely give birth. The commission concluded Israel is guilty of "the crime against humanity of extermination," and its report featured extensive testimony from Palestinian victims detailing rape and sexual torture. The report also accuses Israel of targeted reproductive violence against Palestinians. Sexual violence has long been a feature of Israeli forces' occupation of Palestine, Chris Sidoti, an international human rights lawyer who serves on the commission and co-wrote the report, told me for my reporting in *Jezebel* in March 2025. "It can only be described as systematic, at this point, and it's far more intense now than what was experienced [before October 7]," he said.[10]

When Defense for Children–Palestine informed the US government that a thirteen-year-old Palestinian boy had been raped by an Israeli jail guard, Israel immediately shut down the organization's office and declared it "a terrorist entity."[11] The party that shined light on and challenged abuse, rather than the party that perpetrated the abuse, faced punishment. Under the logic of DARVO, challenging rather than perpetrating abuse renders someone the abuser.

Appallingly enough, pro-Israel propaganda and Western media have devotedly propelled narratives of a supposed mass, coordinated rape campaign perpetrated by Hamas against Israeli women on October 7, weaponizing these narratives to bolster global support for the genocide and capitalize on racist, Western stereotypes about Arab men as caricatured barbarians. President Joe Biden declared at the same time that "it's on all of us" to "forcefully condemn the sexual violence of Hamas terrorists without equivocation—without equivocation, without exception."[12]

There is, of course, zero evidence of any coordinated "mass rape" operation against Israelis perpetrated by Hamas on October 7, or ever. There is, however, extensive, horrific evidence of systematic rape and sexual torture perpetrated by Israel against Palestinians.

In 2023, for plainly stating, in front of the whole world, Israel's war crimes—*including* widespread sexual abuse—Congresswoman Pramila Jayapal faced horrific smears accusing her of condoning sexual assault against Israeli women.[13] Relentless media coverage of unsubstantiated allegations of a mass rape campaign perpetrated by Palestinians, and the emotionally charged political narratives on this matter, are not in good faith. Anyone truly concerned with advocating for sexual violence victims would direct their attention to Israel, whose very existence as a colonial oppressor is an act of gender-based violence. Under colonization and occupation, sexual violence is inescapable.

Yet, to so much as acknowledge any of this, the hegemonic political and cultural powers of the West will smear you as "anti-Semitic," as a rape apologist. Israel and its supporters, meanwhile, are the perpetual victims forced to kill and rape and brutalize ad infinitum, but only in self-defense. "Look what you made me do!" the abuser chastises.

All of this sexual violence against Palestinians, we are told again and again, is either not real, because when a community is as dehumanized in the Western imagination as Palestinians, their suffering does not even register—*or* their suffering is mere collateral from Israel's "self-defense" and, thus, justified. According to Bedera, the language and obfuscation tactics of Israel and its proxies are the mirror image of DARVO. The "toolkit of domination" is present in military conflict and colonization, just as it is in interpersonal abuse.

■ ■ ■

The Depp–Heard trial unfolded about one year into the Biden administration, and the political climate had overwhelmingly become one of complacency—as expected. "Nothing would fundamentally change," then-candidate Joe Biden assured his wealthy donors in 2019.[14] That was his pitch to oust Donald Trump, a serially accused rapist and sexual assailant, a smug authoritarian who has gleefully convinced large swaths of the nation that immigrants and trans people are our collective oppressors, that immigrants and trans people are to blame for the destruction and suffering inflicted on all of us by billionaires like him. That was Biden's pitch: that he would perhaps be more polite and less crass than Trump, but the material differences would be minuscule.

Under Biden, the Supreme Court overturned *Roe v. Wade*, and the administration's response largely amounted to a sad-face emoji. The Democratic Party largely conceded to Trumpian rhetoric and sweeping, dehumanizing political attacks on and scapegoating of immigrants, embracing border militarization and deportations. Anti-trans cruelty proliferated across state legislatures, costs of living continued to soar, right-wing actors launched wildly successful cultural panics blaming all the world's crises on women in the workplace and LGBTQ people, and all of this went largely unchallenged by liberal politicians. Instead, the Biden administration's only real, unwavering position seemed to be, toward the end of his presidency, a commitment to facilitating Israel's genocide in Gaza. Until the end, Biden and his State Department backed the genocide to the hilt, all while fecklessly, pathetically claiming to be working tirelessly behind the scenes to broker a ceasefire—an impossible outcome when the administration unconditionally armed and bankrolled said genocide. In the first months of the second Trump administration in 2025, internal reports surfaced that, actually, Israel faced no real pressure whatsoever from the Biden administration to reach a ceasefire agreement.

Imperialism—the basest, most overt form of domination and political subjugation, the sweeping oppression of other nations through militarism, economic exploitation, and systematic denial of self-determination—is bipartisan in the United States and the West. State and administrative violence, the life-or-death consequences and harms rendered by laws and policies, is bipartisan, too. But to those in power, challenges to these dynamics are the real abuse.

Oppressive systems persist in no small part through an appalling performance of victimhood and powerlessness—the most effective form of propaganda. Those in power maintain their power by misrepresenting their victims' resistance as the only aggression taking place, necessitating a forceful response that maintains the status quo of oppression. Across the board in American society, there is a distinct lack of political literacy about what violence entails and the structural forms that it takes. Thus, this DARVO-based propaganda is ultra-effective.

Consider the Trump administration's treatment of legal US resident Kilmar Abrego Garcia in 2025, illegally sending Abrego Garcia to a brutal, high-security prison in El Salvador by error, then justifying this by casting him as an imperfect victim.[15] In many ways, the shameless cruelty of Abrego Garcia's case is a microcosm for the administration's broader approach to governing, by brazenly wielding the tactics of domestic abusers to enact its authoritarian agenda. At the heart of the second Trump administration's unapologetic fascism are the same gendered, patriarchal behaviors of abusers.

It should come as no surprise that an administration staffed from top to bottom with accused abusers would prioritize policies that enact state violence and carry disparate, targeted harm for victims and survivors. This includes defunding family planning programs, gutting a federal agency tasked with preventing intimate partner violence, enacting a range of anti-survivor campus sexual assault measures, and threatening incarcerated trans women with state-sanctioned rape by trying to send them to men's prisons. Trump's rhetoric to justify all of these actions relies on self-victimization and distortion, framing the most marginalized as the real abusive figures.

DARVO is baked into the DNA of the Trump administration—but DARVO is also baked into the imperialist project of the United States writ large.

To begin, this book places particular focus on the case study of Israel–Palestine—around which both major American political parties operate in lockstep with each other—and the decades-long American Zionist campaign to frame Israel's genocidal war on Palestine as "self-defense." Zionists aggressively wield sexual atrocity propaganda to obscure how Israel itself is a perpetrator of mass sexual violence—just as all colonizing forces have been throughout history, because sexual violence is a tool of colonization. All of this directly mirrors the gaslighting, manipulation, exploitation of power dynamics, and direct physical violence characteristic of abusive situations; this has always been true of imperialist aggression. To construct these arguments, I draw on hours of interviews with humanitarian workers, human rights lawyers, doctors, attorneys representing Palestinian sexual assault survivors, and sexual violence researchers.

This book further examines parallels to DARVO and other abusive tactics within numerous case studies of state violence and oppression.

In the US legal system, abusers sue, bankrupt, and crush victims who speak out. With increasingly violent fervor, the US immigration system sweepingly characterizes immigrants as violent rapists to justify policies that further victimize them, demolish the civil rights of people of all immigration statuses, and enact exponentially greater harm on abuse victims in immigrant communities. The anti-abortion movement wields the conceit of embryos and fetuses as victims of "murder" to justify the state torture and killing of pregnant people.

To conclude, I review and examine historical revolutionary violence, and neoliberal respectability politics and policing of modes of resistance to oppression. I also explore different perspectives on revolutionary violence as self-defense, and the political theater and manipulation that determine who must condemn which acts of violence, and which acts of violence are accepted, even honored, as the norm.

Our oppressors justify the full gamut of state violence through the performance of victimhood, not unlike domestic abusers. Consequently, we must turn to key tenets of survivor justice and victim advocacy to guide our resistance. That means unconditional advocacy for victims of abuse and state violence and oppression—regardless of their pasts or the circumstances leading up to the abuse they face from the state. That means abandoning innately gendered, white supremacist notions of what makes someone a perfect or worthy victim. That means questioning who those in power frame as abusers and questioning structural power imbalances. And it also means recognizing that marginalized people are often treated as threats to the state for simply existing—notions of traditional respectability will get us nowhere.

Fascism is inextricably linked to gender-based violence and the playbook of abusers. In response, we must rely on the compassionate, unflinching playbook of survivor justice to fight back and build toward something better.

1

THE RIGHT TO SELF-DEFENSE

You are a person who a crime has been committed against, but somehow you are on trial, find yourself in cross-examination about crimes committed against you.

—MOHAMMED EL-KURD

Do you know why I hate Hamas? Because it forces my children to kill Palestinian children.

—HAI BAR-EL, Tel Aviv

You don't mean peace talks. You mean capitulation, surrendering. "Why not just talk?" Talk to whom?

—GHASSAN KANAFANI

Look what you made me do.
I was just defending myself.
You gave me no choice.

In 1970 Ghassan Kanafani, a spokesperson for the Popular Front for the Liberation of Palestine (PFLP), sat down for an interview with journalist Richard Carleton.[1] In the interview, Carleton repeatedly asks Kanafani why the PFLP doesn't simply conduct "peace talks" with the Israeli apartheid regime to prevent hostilities, all as regime-backed Israeli settlers bulldozed Palestinian villages and displaced, imprisoned, and murdered Palestinians in droves on their own land.

"Why not talk?" Carleton repeats throughout the conversation. "Why not talk?"

"You don't mean exactly peace talks. You mean capitulation, surrendering. 'Why not just talk?' Talk to whom?" Kanafani initially responds.

"Talk to the Israeli leaders," Carleton says.

To this, Kanafani aptly replies, "That's the kind of conversation between the sword and the neck."

Not registering this, or rather, refusing to conceptualize the bureaucratic and administrative execution of state violence, with or without the physical presence of guns, Carleton says, "If there were no swords and no guns in the room, you could still talk." Eventually, Carleton argues that "peace talks" could "stop the fighting, stop the death and the misery, the destruction, the pain."

"The misery and the destruction and the pain and the death of whom?" Kanafani asks.

"Of Palestinians, of Israelis, of Arabs," says Carleton.

"And the Palestinian people who are uprooted, thrown in the camps, living in starvation, killed for twenty years, and forbidden to use even the name Palestinians?" Kanafani asks.

"Better that way than dead," Carleton says.

Kanafani roundly rejects this: "Maybe to you, but to us, it's not. To us, to liberate our country, to have dignity, to have respect, to have our mere human rights, is something as essential as life itself."

Two years later, the Israeli regime assassinated Kanafani and his seventeen-year-old niece with a bomb placed under his car,[2] shredding their bodies to pieces.

Ghassan Kanafani was a much, much better person than I. I would not have been able to sit with a straight face while a person who had never been displaced by settlers insisted that I simply "talk" to the people who hold the power of life or death over me and my family. Kanafani's eventual fate speaks to precisely why this interview was so nauseating. Nevertheless, Kanafani remained calm and levelheaded throughout the conversation. In the same ways that rape and abuse victims must earn and audition for credibility and public trust, while their rapists and abusers are born with it, this too is the dynamic of colonizers and the colonized.

Why not talk? Why not talk?

Watching the conversation, from start to finish, I could only think of the abuse victims I've interviewed throughout my career who faced criminal charges or other forms of state-sanctioned punishment and condemnation for resisting or fighting back against their abusers. I'll never forget my conversation with a woman whose husband routinely, brutally beat her so often that she suffered a string of miscarriages. When she eventually related this to the police, she says one officer told her that spousal rape and abuse aren't real, because the wife is an appendage of her husband, and a man cannot beat himself. Nor will I forget the woman who tried to report her rape to the police to prevent her rapist from gaining shared custody of her son; police interrogated her for all of two days, she said, while they questioned her rapist for thirty minutes. They let him go, and effectively trapped her in a decade-long, existential custody battle with her abuser by refusing to charge him.[3]

Why don't women in these scenarios simply "talk" to the towering men who slam their faces onto the ground and stomp on their heads? Why don't these women simply "talk" to the men who own guns and have unilateral access to their children?

These questions are insulting, appalling, an affront to the very notion of human dignity. But these are the very questions that Palestinians—who inconvenience the Western world by not rolling over and dying—are asked, every single day. These are the questions that Carleton posed to Kanafani, two years before Israel murdered him alongside a child.

At the core of Carleton's questions lies the feel-good, infantile, liberal fantasy that violence can simply and tidily be resolved with nonviolence, that those who respond to violence *with* violence are ever-so-casually making a choice rather than trying to survive. No person is born to be oppressed, and it's human nature for oppression to be met with resistance. In 2024, I spoke with sexual violence researcher Dr. Nicole Bedera about her work examining how universities treat reported campus sexual assaults by observing one school's Title IX office throughout 2019; she found that due to fear of being perceived as biased in favor of victims at the height of the MeToo movement, school officials were desperate to perform neutrality in ways that were so crushing to victims, many had to drop out of school altogether.[4] That's because "there's a huge power disparity between victim and perpetrator," Bedera told me. "If you treat victim and perpetrator the same, you will always be enabling the perpetrator and empowering them to have more power over the victim."

Under rape culture as well as the logics of imperialism, there is a total erasure of power dynamics, a sweeping neutralization of the reasons why two sides are fighting, and what would happen if either side stopped. "End the violence and just talk," Palestinians are told. "Stop the fighting, stop the death and the misery, the destruction, the pain," Carleton said to Kanafani.

If Israel stopped fighting, millions would be liberated and innumerable lives would be saved. An entire population would be able to live with dignity and self-determination, children across Palestine would no longer be shot by snipers and sexually abused in jails, hospitals would no longer be bombed, and people could return to their homes and move freely from one place to another. If Palestinians stopped fighting, they would die.

If rapists stopped raping, rape would stop. I cannot even imagine, meanwhile, what the world would look like if survivors stopped trying to survive.

In 2021, Palestinian resistance leader Yahya Sinwar gave his last formal interview. He was asked to justify Hamas attacks on Israel that sometimes kill civilians. In response, Sinwar raised that Israel kills Palestinian civilians en masse despite having access to the advanced technologies that could prevent such killings—Palestinians do not. Sinwar's death in 2024 exemplifies this reality: Israel killed him with the use of advanced drone technology—after well over a year of bombing hospital after hospital, refugee camp after refugee camp, shrugging an entire genocide off as an inevitable "oopsie" because, Israel claimed, this was collateral damage as they supposedly targeted Hamas officials.

"Does the world expect us to be well-behaved victims while we are being killed, for us to be slaughtered without making a noise?" Sinwar said in the 2021 interview.[5] "We decided to defend our people with whatever weapons we have."

Sinwar was born in a refugee camp—as so many Palestinians are—in Gaza in 1962. His parents had been forcibly displaced by Israeli settlers in 1948 during the Nakba, which saw Israel expel and murder close to one million Palestinians. Sinwar rose to political power first as a student activist, who was eventually jailed by Israel for more than twenty years; in 2018, he helped lead the Great March of Return protests, during which Israel killed at least 230 peaceful protesters.

That—mass murder—was Israel's response to Palestinians who tried to "talk."

That same year, a journalist asked Sinwar what he thought of Israel's classification of him as a terrorist: "And that's what they are for me," he said. The journalist responded that such comments from him would sabotage a ceasefire. Sinwar said:

> And what should I say? We hit civilians? They hit civilians. They suffered? We suffered. Tell me about any of their dead, and I

> will tell you of one of our dead. Of ten of our dead. And so? That's why you are here? You are here to talk of the dead, or to avoid new casualties? But most of all, you. Do you think you are innocent, only because you are Italian—neither Arab nor Jewish? How easy it is for you to come from far away and feel wise and fair. We all have blood on our hands. You too. Where were you during these 11 years of siege? And during these 50 years of occupation? Where were you?[6]

He continued, "I am not saying I won't fight anymore. . . . I am saying that I don't want war anymore. You walk to the beach at sunset, and you see all these teenagers on the shore chatting and wondering what the world looks like across the sea. What life looks like. It's breaking. And should break everybody. I want them free."

Under imperialism, as under patriarchy, only one side *can* end the violence by ceasing to fight. The other can only concede and die.

■ ■ ■

Israel does not have a right to defend itself. Israel does not have a right to exist. States do not have a right to exist, borders do not have a right to exist—people have a right to exist. And people have a right to *resist*, to struggle to be free, which is an innate and irrepressible human instinct.

I can't think of a starting point for this book more fundamental than that simple statement of fact. No state has a right to exist, and certainly not Israel, whose existence has always been premised on genocide. People have a right to live on any land safe from apartheid, starvation, rape, displacement, genocide, and any of the other great, innumerable war crimes perpetrated by Israel against Palestinians for decades now, all bankrolled and armed by the United States and other Western, imperialist superpowers. *That*—the human right to live, to exist, to be free—takes precedence over any state's existence. This is true when applied to borders and immigration laws, too: The very notion that you or I or anyone should be able to decide where other human beings can or can't live, where they can or can't move, is preposterous enough on its face. Held to the light, further exposed by the endless man-made tragedies, the wars, deaths, famines, and family separations, that notion is exponentially more preposterous. I have no sources to cite for any of these claims except for my own humanity, a lifetime of watching borders destroy, dehumanize, and birth new, hateful worlds out of blood and partitions.

Israel's very existence is predicated on, inseparable from, that notion of who can live where, of which humans, which children, have a right to live and exist, have a right to grow old. Israel doesn't have a right to exist nor "defend" its existence against a captive population. But captive populations, like Palestinians across occupied Palestine, have an absolute right to defend themselves from their occupiers who enforce their rule through terror.

That refrain—Israel has a right to defend itself—goes entirely unchallenged, upheld as sacred in the canon of American politics. It's the pretext for billions of dollars in weapons the United States sends to Israel annually. We're told that funding for Israel's Iron Dome, the security system that intercepts missiles, is "defensive" spending, that even if you don't support Israel's illegal occupation and the Gaza genocide, surely you support the defense of Israeli civilians. "Iron Dome is a purely defensive system that protects civilians. It saves lives, regardless of religion or ethnicity," then-Senator Bob Menendez, a Democrat, declared in 2021:

> Furthermore, by saving those lives, Iron Dome also preserves diplomatic space for deescalation, communication, and further negotiations about Israeli and Palestinian long-term security and the future of a negotiated two-state solution.[7]

But why should any moral country send any kind of aid, whatever label is attached to it, to reward and uphold an apartheid regime committing genocide? Even sending supposedly "defensive" weapons, a misnomer, subsidizes Israel's ability to continue the wholesale slaughter of a captive population and further insulates Israel from the threat of consequences or retaliation that could curb the genocide. The Jerusalem-based journalist Nathan Thrall told *Jewish Currents* in 2023 that "in theory, a weapon like Iron Dome could be used only defensively. But in practice it doesn't work that way" because the "Iron Dome facilitates greater Israeli offensive measures, because it lowers the perceived cost to Israel of escalating or extending or initiating attacks."[8]

As Palestinian Jewish writer Dylan Saba wrote in *Jewish Currents* in 2023, the Iron Dome "cannot meaningfully be considered 'life-saving' in any value system that recognizes Palestinian humanity." He further wrote that by "depriving Palestinians of even the most limited means of military deterrence, the US has given Israel a blank check to massacre Gazans," and "by funding a system that guarantees their acts of resistance are of almost no consequence to their oppressors, we are consigning them to death." He explained further:

> By almost entirely negating the ability of militant groups in Gaza to respond to Israel's incursions, the purportedly defensive Iron Dome allows Israel to strike without fear of repercussion. And because the cost is so low when measured in Israeli casualties, Israel can wage perpetual war without suffering domestic political consequences, and is under negligible pressure to pursue diplomacy with the Palestinians.

Helping Israel defend itself cannot be understood as a peaceful, nonviolent, or fair and equal approach to the so-called "conflict" between Israel and Palestine. This is because Israel's existence as an apartheid state and occupying force is not peaceful, nor nonviolent, nor fair, nor equal. As the writer and scholar Mary Turfah wrote in an essay in 2024: "The framework of 'pro-Palestine' versus 'pro-Israel' feels deceptive: these aren't horizontal enemies but mutually exclusive realities—oppressor and oppressed—where only one 'side' exists literally on top of the other's graves."[9]

To condemn Israel is a moral necessity. But all too often, those who condemn Israel's genocidal actions are then pressured to condemn a wide range of irrelevant or overtly nonsensical things that undermine who holds power in the situation, and the root cause and perpetrator of the crisis. They are pressured to condemn paramilitary resistance groups, condemn ethnic and therefore scary slogans, condemn nineteen-year-old college students who pitch tents on campus to protest genocide. In 2025, the Democratic Socialist state Assemblyman Zohran Mamdani ran for mayor of New York City. Despite Mamdani's wide-ranging platform and his plans for universal childcare and lowered costs of living, journalists rarely asked him any questions beyond whether he condemned the slogan "globalize the Intifada," or whether he believed Israel has a right to exist.

These are fundamentally unserious demands. Anyone who is serious about condemning violence and destruction will trace it to its root. In the case of Israel–Palestine, the root is Israel.

The urgent demand for anyone who expresses support for Palestine to condemn the Palestinian resistance, to criticize the colonized for how they respond to their oppression, is all too familiar to survivors and advocates for survivor justice. These demands reflect how we criticize and cross-examine victims of abuse over their responses to that abuse. All too often, when someone critiques the behaviors of victims, the insinuation is that under those same conditions, they would be better, they would find some peaceful way to escape with their life intact. To condemn something is to say that you, under those same circumstances, would not do what they did.

That is patently absurd. No one with access to water in their homes, the ability to move from one place to another freely, to go to a hospital without that hospital being bombed, to not have family members killed by an occupying army, could possibly say what they would or would not do, what measures they would or would not take to try to be free.

This was the context in which I was first introduced to Israel and Palestine, while organizing for survivor justice on my college campus. Connecting with student organizers at my school's Students for Justice in Palestine, I was struck by the similarities in victim-blaming language and tactics aimed at victims of sexual violence, and at Palestinians who resisted their Israeli oppressors. And I was struck, too, by Israelis' systematic use of sexual violence against captive Palestinian populations as a means to further consolidate power.

Less than a year after Hamas forces launched their offensive against Israel on October 7, 2023, *The Lancet* journal published a study estimating that roughly 200,000 Palestinians in Gaza had been killed—by bombs, airstrikes, famine, disease, torture, captivity.[10] Israel's genocidal campaign on the Gaza Strip—a blockaded, twenty-five-by-six-mile strip of land with a population of about two million—has not stopped as I write this in 2025. That genocidal campaign has entailed endless bombardment, killing an estimated 200,000 within a year and injuring and trapping thousands more under rubble. Through all of this barbarism, US politicians, Zionist organizations, and the highly influential Israel lobby have parroted out the same refrain while funding Israel's war crimes: "Israel has a right to defend itself." It doesn't matter to American politicians, or the Israel lobby, that aggression from the occupier cannot in good faith be understood as "self-defense." Nevertheless, Israel, per the overwhelming majority of US politicians, is the victim, and the Palestinians that Israel is occupying are the aggressor.

But the ongoing realities on the ground are perhaps best encapsulated by a dispatch from United Nations Children's Fund (UNICEF) officer James Elder, who told *The New Yorker* of a recent visit to Gaza in the summer of 2025:

> There were burns on little girls and boys, fourth-degree burns I didn't know existed. And shrapnel riddled through a body.

> Shrapnel is designed to go through cement, and what it does to a child's body is horrific. On one previous trip, I saw a bus of children who spent two days trying to get from the north to the south after being held at Israeli checkpoints, and I walked in the bus, and all I could smell was children's burning flesh. It doesn't leave you. And one of the things that struck me this time was that I wasn't just seeing these children—I was hearing them. There is such a horrendous lack of painkillers that when I'd be in a hospital—and hospitals are wall to wall with people with wounds of war—you'd hear the children and their screams.[11]

Yet, no matter how many civilians Israel kills in Gaza, it never seems to matter to the imperialist powers that could end the genocide with a phone call. Murder is a necessity, Israel says, because Palestinian militants use human shields. But, foremost, if this were true, is it not more barbaric to utterly disregard the "human shields" in question and indiscriminately slaughter the so-called "shields" anyway? Secondly, we have seen time and again that it's the Israeli army that routinely and systematically uses human shields, as Palestinian victims recount being detained, beaten, tortured, and then trotted out while Israeli soldiers hide behind them.

It's often repeated that every accusation deployed by Israel's propaganda machine is a confession—and it can't be repeated enough. In any case, there are no Palestinian civilians in the Zionist imagination, because everyone in Gaza is "Hamas"—civil servants, government aid workers, citizens who may or may not have voted to elect Hamas officials—everyone and everything in Israel's way is "Hamas," everyone and everything in Israel's way is unworthy of life. By 2024, Israel determined that UNRWA, the United Nations Relief and Works Agency for Palestine Refugees in the Near East, was Hamas, a conclusion that appears to have been reached largely through kidnapping and torturing aid workers. Consequently, the United States defunded UNRWA and replaced the agency with a sham, privatized humanitarian relief organization called the Gaza

Humanitarian Foundation, effectively run by Israeli forces alongside the Boston Consulting Group. The so-called Gaza Humanitarian Foundation alone was allowed to enter Gaza with aid. But its aid sites were death traps that lured starving, dying Palestinians in with bags of flour—some reportedly laced with opioids—to be shot and killed. As many as 100 Palestinians were killed at these so-called aid sites within a month in the summer of 2025.[12]

Hamas, an armed political party founded in 1987, is an acronym for Harakat al-Muqawama al-Islamiyya (the Islamic Resistance Movement). In Arabic, the word translates to "zeal." Hamas won elections to helm the Palestinian Authority in Gaza and the occupied West Bank in 2006. The party differs from the Palestine Liberation Organization (PLO) and the Palestinian Authority (PA), as Hamas does not recognize the state of Israel and declared in its 2017 political charter, "Resisting the occupation with all means and methods is a legitimate right guaranteed by divine laws and by international norms and laws. At the heart of these lies armed resistance."[13] In late 2025, a ceasefire agreement between Israel and Hamas, facilitated by the Trump administration, required Hamas to forfeit political power in Gaza.

"There will be no electricity, no food, no water, no fuel, everything will be closed. We are fighting against human animals and will act accordingly," Israeli Defense Minister Yoav Gallant said on October 9, 2023, to justify Israel's comprehensive blockade on Gaza.[14] It should have spoken volumes about who victim and oppressor were and are, based on who had the unilateral power to enshrine and enforce such a blockade, and, certainly, based on who referred to their enemy as "animals." The violence and brutality from Israeli forces only continued to escalate after Gallant's comments: Palestinian doctors and aid workers detained by the Israeli military and executed one by one;[15] prisoners detained for being Palestinian, tortured, and, in at least one case, raped to death by Israeli soldiers;[16] a constant influx of "children's heads smashed to pieces" by American bullets, as at least one American doctor who served in Gaza told reporters in the summer of 2024;[17] a constant influx of orphaned children, limbless children, children's charred remains.

"Do you know why I hate Hamas? Because it forces my children to kill Palestinian children," the self-identified Israeli human rights attorney Hai Bar-El told the *Financial Times* in October 2024, from the safety of his home in Tel Aviv.[18]

Golda Meir, the fourth prime minister of Israel, said in 1969, "We can forgive the Arabs for killing our children. But we can never forgive them for forcing us to kill their children."[19]

Look what you made me do, says the abuser. *I was just defending myself. You gave me no choice.*

■ ■ ■

Palestinian writer Mohammed El-Kurd's work has often brought to life the politics of victimhood in the imperialist imagination. His writing is fearless in its critiques of the ways that victims of imperialism are dehumanized even by those who claim to support them, only to condemn them should they resist or fight back against their oppressors in any way. His arguments are essential reading for allies of the Palestinian, anti-imperialist cause to question our modes of advocacy.

In 2025, I interviewed El-Kurd about his new book, *Perfect Victims*, for a review in *Jezebel* shortly before his book came out. I was particularly struck by some of the parallels he drew between the treatment of rape and abuse victims under patriarchy and the treatment of Palestine and the colonized world under imperialism.[20] Telling Palestinian stories to a mainstream audience, El-Kurd argues in *Perfect Victims*, seems to require the endless, impossible performance of innocence and respectability, with perpetrators never named and passive voice deployed at all times. It requires titular "perfect victims" who can never be the protagonists even in their own stories. But "perfect victims" don't exist.[21] El-Kurd's book excoriates the absurd politics of how colonized people are supposed to appeal to their colonizers and deconstructs how even those who are sympathetic to Palestine rely on dehumanizing talking points about Palestinians to advocate for them, in a world that treats Palestinians' desire for freedom as innately more dangerous and violent than bombs and genocide. As its name suggests, El-Kurd's book is also a detailed exploration of how victimhood is both assigned and erased, and its limitations under imperialism, reminding me of generations of feminist thinkers who have exposed the fundamentally impossible ways that victims are forced to audition for credibility and justice under patriarchy.

As a child, El-Kurd remembers when journalists would visit his home in Sheikh Jarrah, a neighborhood in Jerusalem, in the early 2010s, as Israeli settlers increasingly displaced families like his. Many of these settlers hailed from Brooklyn and were sponsored or financed by various tax-deductible American nonprofit organizations. El-Kurd writes about Western journalists' fascination with documenting the mass suffering and loss inflicted on his community, sometimes interviewing children like him. But they were never interested in much more than that—in children's suffering, that is. They weren't interested in Palestinians' political analysis about their own plight and oppression, because the "conflict," as the decades-long ethnic cleansing of Palestinians is often gently labeled, was somehow far too complicated for the people experiencing it to be able to credibly speak about. And they weren't interested in the voices of adults, who might hold anger toward the settlers who looted their homes, destroyed their furniture in the streets, and kidnapped and jailed their children without charge. The adults' anger rendered them imperfect victims.

Early in *Perfect Victims*, El-Kurd addresses the weaponization of gender amid Israel's genocide in Gaza, the outsized focus on its impacts on women and children, and the qualifiers that are often required for Palestinian men to be seen as worthy of life, too: Men have to be loving grandfathers, or selfless doctors, or cry out as they carry their children's dead bodies on camera for all the world to see their pain. In many, seemingly contradictory ways, gender has and hasn't mattered amid the genocide. "Bombs don't discriminate, they don't spare women and children—it's a wholesale targeting," El-Kurd told me in our conversation.

Under the Israeli occupation, boys "are men and girls are men and women are men, too," he writes in *Perfect Victims*, referencing a famous line from the Irish poet Padraic Fiacc. There is no childhood for Palestinian children, for girls subjected to routine sexual assault by Israeli soldiers performing body searches at checkpoints, or boys routinely detained and jailed without charge under administrative detention, who come of age "under the moon of fluorescent lighting in the interrogation room," El-Kurd writes. He further reflects on how the global community is desensitized to Palestinian suffering, indiscriminately:

> We die in fleeting headlines, in between breaths. Our death is so quotidian that journalists report it as though they're reporting the weather: *Cloudy skies, light showers, and 3,000 Palestinians dead in the past ten days*. And much like the weather, only God is responsible—not armed settlers, not targeted drone strikes. Our massacres are only interrupted by commercial breaks. Judges legalize them. Correspondents kill us with passive voice. If we are lucky, diplomats say that our death concerns them, but they never mention the culprit, let alone condemn the culprit.

Despite this lack of distinction, gender remains an important marker in cultural discourse about the Gaza genocide. Women are accorded victimhood in the popular imagination, El-Kurd says, and yet, not only has this failed to spare them from suffering, but it's also "reduced them to sticks in the wind, robbed them of agency, erased their very active role in the Palestinian struggle." As for Palestinian men, "We're told, 'Don't forget men, they're gentle fathers, this and that,' but there shouldn't be a characteristic anyone needs to embody to be deserving of dignity and liberation."

At one point in *Perfect Victims*, El-Kurd observes how victims must be "sanitized and subdued" before anyone can possibly sympathize with them: "One could say the same about sexual assault victims: we must notify the listener that the victim was sober and dressed appropriately." This reminds me, again, of the numerous comparisons between political discourse about the Palestinian struggle and the tactics of domestic abusers. There's DARVO, which we see when every strike on a school in Gaza is justified by Israel's "right to defend itself," or we're told that a hospital is actually a Hamas military base. And there's "orchestrated complexity," the manufacturing of nuance and conditions that always benefit the abuser, often achieved by starting in the middle of an abusive situation, when a victim resists or responds to abuse. In *Perfect Victims*, El-Kurd describes this as the phenomenon of "secondly": "We accept starting the story at 'secondly.' But . . . before I threw the rock, they stole my land. Before I picked up the rifle, they shot my loved ones. Before I made the makeshift rocket, they put me in a cage."

Consider the news reports about the genocide in Gaza that start with October 7, or the condemnations of Palestinians for throwing rocks at soldiers, or, in Palestinian intellectual Edward Said's case, throwing a pebble at an Israeli military watchtower—we never hear about why soldiers or guard towers or other vestiges of militarization and occupation are there in the first place. "We never want to tackle things at the root or ask what started this—we're angry at symptoms but not the disease, which is colonialism and occupation," El-Kurd told me. "The discourse is so regressive that people refuse to see resistance as a reaction to something, as a survival mechanism."

The subjugation of Palestinians under imperialism holds parallels to not just rape culture discourse, but also treatment of victims of police brutality, El-Kurd told me. In 2014, an Israeli airstrike killed four

Palestinian boys playing soccer on the beach, and El-Kurd recounted watching as Israeli spokespeople went on TV to question why they were on the beach and if they were members of Hamas. "You are a person who a crime has been committed against, but somehow *you* are on trial, find yourself in cross-examination about crimes committed against *you*," El-Kurd said. "To shift blame from perpetrator to victim, this has all the parallels to sexual assault victims, police brutality victims."

Israeli statehood itself is often justified by the fundamentally racist premise that Palestinians and Arabs are innately born wishing to kill all Jewish people. Since October 2023, Israeli soldiers have claimed to find obviously planted copies of *Mein Kampf* in Palestinian children's nurseries. "The hatred we supposedly possess, lurking within our hearts, receives more concern than the nuclear arsenal of our colonizers," El-Kurd writes. That's why the first pages of *Perfect Victims* state, in big, sprawling letters, "*even if*." This, he said, is the central thesis of the book: *Even if* every worst circumstance and characterization that Israel has invented about Palestinians is true, that could never justify occupation, apartheid, and genocide. *Even if* racist tropes about Palestinian soldiers wielding "human shields" were true, that could never justify bombing hospitals.

Also in *Perfect Victims*, El-Kurd presents an apt metaphor comparing US politicians and one-sided Western media coverage to the violence of snipers:

> The dehumanizers are not only the vulgar right-wingers . . . but the most politically correct of killers who deny us even eye contact before they pull the trigger, sniping coldly, impersonally, from hundreds of meters away. . . . The snipers are everywhere: the underhanded journalists, the spineless bureaucrats, the television anchors who obfuscate those tragedies. The sniper's hands are clean of blood, but his body count is insurmountable.

It's a "hard task," he said, "to get people to see violence as a more complex, structural mechanism." For example, gender-based violence is often understood solely as rape and domestic violence, not abortion bans, or a privatized health care system that forces rape victims to pay for medical care out of pocket. In a similar vein, most people are conditioned to see "violence orchestrated by Joe Biden or Donald Trump or [former Secretary of State] Antony Blinken as something other than violence—as management, bureaucracy, a necessary fact of life," El-Kurd said. Many only see informal militias, or middle-aged Palestinian men "in tracksuits and flip-flops" throwing rocks, as violent. With *Perfect Victims*, El-Kurd hopes to "challenge a person's understanding and definition of violence," he told me. "I argue those people in suits, who speak with such sophisticated, polite language, know all the etiquette, are the biggest threats to humanity. To me, hunger is violence, not being able to afford health care is violence, not feeling safe [under occupation] is violence—it's not just a punch and slap, but policies, laws, legislation."

Perfect Victims is rife with similar frameworks that challenge even those supportive of the Palestinian cause to question their approaches to advocacy. El-Kurd interrogates why we so often see Israeli sources, such as journalists or other individuals who have "miraculous epiphanies" about Israel's cruelty and criticize Israel, or refuse to join the army, prioritized over Palestinian voices. He interrogates the "fetishization" of Israeli–Palestinian collaborations in documentaries and storytelling projects, while work exclusively created by Palestinians is sidelined: "It comes off to me as satisfying this selfish urge in audiences to see reconciliation between slayer and slain take place on-screen, because it's not taking place in real life," he said, joking that this "reminds me of how, growing up, most of the feminist literature I first read in school was written by men." But it's not feminist for even ostensibly enlightened men to speak for women, nor is it liberation for Israelis to speak for Palestinians.

El-Kurd writes toward the end of *Perfect Victims*, "I don't know what to do with brutality except to laugh at it." His book is rife with horrific accounts of brutality, examples of Israeli soldiers branding

Palestinians' faces with the Star of David, of journalists and children killed by Israeli soldiers with impunity—only for their loved ones to then be killed by soldiers at the subsequent funerals. But *Perfect Victims* is also interspersed with sharp humor, as El-Kurd responds to bad-faith and absurd questions about Palestinians' alleged, natural-born desire to kill Jewish people and the supposed genocide they'd inflict on Israelis if they received freedom: "I am often asked if I want to 'throw Israelis into the sea.' . . . If they are so afraid of drowning why don't they learn how to swim?" he writes.

"It's a ridiculous thing, Palestinians being bombed and burned alive, and you're asking me what's going to happen in the future, hypothetically—that's ridiculous, and we should treat it as such," El-Kurd told me. "We're asked these hypotheticals as if they're sacred questions we should all bow before. Humor and irreverence expose what these questions really are." Writing in *The Nation* in 2025, he expanded on some of these thoughts—particularly the idea that, again, by wishing for freedom, he wishes to drown Israelis in the sea:

> Colonial logic says that if I were to have that mere desire within my heart; if I am fantasizing about cartoonish revenges, that alone negates my claim to justice. Thus, any testimony of the injustices I have witnessed and endured is unreliable. The brutality of colonialism, the very brutality that is institutionalized and legalized, can then be excused or even warranted, if I were to want such a turn of events. Such desires, according to mind-reading critics, linger deep within our psyche and should discredit the Palestinian. . . . To simply imagine Palestine without settlers, to simply imagine a sky without drones—that, in the Zionist imagination, is genocidal. If you stick with the "want" of the charge, the notion that Palestinians want to kill all Jews, you find that Zionism is at war with our future. It is at war with our ability to articulate, even if only through poems and protest chants, a future in which Zionism does not reign.[22]

Perfect Victims is an exploration of how powerless and powerful we all are to resist Zionism, all at the same time, and the simultaneous uselessness and inescapability of our feelings of guilt living in a world ravaged by colonialism. One of the book's central contradictions, El-Kurd told me, is serving as "a critique of the politics of appeal, while being an appeal itself." While the book examines Palestinian suffering and the erasure of that suffering across the West, its thesis is one of dignity: "We [Palestinians] need to live with dignity no matter what," he said. "That means refusal to stand trial, be cross-examined—even if the worst you say about me is true, you have no right to steal my land, to oppress me, to erase me."

This right of refusal, the paradigm of "even if," together present a sweeping challenge to Zionism and abusers writ large. There is an innate human need to be free; no one is born to be oppressed, to live in a cage. Victims—of interpersonal gender-based violence as well as colonial violence—will resist and defend themselves.

And their resistance in no way changes who the victim and offender are.

■ ■ ■

In late 2023, I spoke at length with Dr. Bedera about the language and obfuscation tactics that the US pro-Israel lobby deploys to justify their cause of relentless genocide, all in the name of Israel's supposed victimhood. These tactics have long felt achingly familiar, reminding me of my reporting on gender-based violence. The Zionist project and its supporters appear to take their cues from the behaviors and conceits of abusers. In particular, Dr. Bedera and I were reminded of DARVO: deny, attack, reverse victim and offender. The "toolkit of domination" isn't just applied interpersonally, she said. It also applies to military conflict and colonization.

"Victims are not allowed to defend themselves from the abuser," Bedera told me for my reporting in *Prism*.[23] When they do, they're "cast as the aggressor, especially by the criminal justice system," and often face criminal charges for acts of self-defense. "Aggressors will try to make themselves look like the victim, to make any violence from them 'self-defense,' and any violence from their victim into an act of aggression. There's only one group that's permitted to be violent and aggressive." This, Bedera argued, is mirrored to a T in Western conceptions of Israel–Palestine.

Bedera also pointed to Israel's targeting of Palestinian journalists in Gaza, killing more than 230 by July 2025 and sometimes killing their entire families, as deliberate. This is an abusive tactic to render it as difficult as possible to disseminate information, to let facts reach people around the world. The killing of journalists, Bedera said, is a "violent denial" of victims' reality. "DARVO is not about convincing the listener what happened, but making both sides seem untrustworthy. It's about convincing people to be neutral, that they don't know what's going on and so they should just look the other way from the abuse."

Jacqueline Cruz, another sexual violence researcher, has titled this tactic of abusers "orchestrated complexity"—the deliberate shrouding of facts, the manufacturing of nuance, qualifications, and conditions that always privilege the abuser. This is how the false narrative of something like "mutual abuse" arises, obscuring who has any power to abuse in the first place. When a situation seems too complicated—even though it isn't actually complicated at all—institutions are able to justify inaction.

This is what Bedera saw all the time in her years of study about how American universities handle—or rather, *don't* handle—endemic campus sexual assault by manipulating federal Title IX policies that govern gender-based discrimination. "With Title IX, the thing they [universities] want to do is nothing. It's the least amount of legal risk, it allows them to protect the perpetrators," Bedera said. Similarly, Bedera told me, she's observed how the widespread, unending dissemination of videos of the on-the-ground horrors in Gaza are often met with ostensibly objective, neutral parties trying to offer context: "It's [always], 'Well, it's more complicated than you think,' and sometimes that may be true. But the result is, it makes people feel like they don't have enough context to take a stand. It doesn't necessarily make them switch sides, but they're afraid to take the wrong side, so they just don't take one." The assumption, Bedera says, is that "inaction is neutral." But it will always benefit the abuser—the person or institution in the position of power, wielding that power to perpetrate harm.

In the vein of "orchestrating complexity," one of the most common tactics deployed by abusers is to revise or obfuscate when a violent situation first began. Consider, for instance, uncritical Western media's obsession with October 7, 2023. "When you start in the middle of a conflict rather than the beginning, you're very unlikely to be able to tell why what just happened took place, or see who the primary aggressor is," Bedera said. "Nothing starts with just a random attack—that's not how this works." October 7 was not the beginning; rather, "the [Israeli] occupation is akin to the beginning of an abusive relationship." And, in both interpersonal and imperialist contexts, victims can find themselves forced to use violence to resist violence.

Obscuring the most basic facts about Israel and Palestine before or after a distorted version of October 7 creates the perfect conditions for the Israel lobby to weaponize DARVO and sanitize the ongoing terrorism and war crimes indiscriminately perpetrated by Israel as "self-defense." The abusive act of "denial" is deeply embedded in the US government's response to every Gaza hospital bombed by Israel and every dialysis patient and premature baby killed by Israel's blockade,[24] and it is also crystallized by President Biden's conspiracy theory in November 2023 that the reported death counts from Gaza's Health Ministry can't be trusted.[25] Consider the outrage that American politicians like Rashida Tlaib and Alexandria Ocasio-Cortez faced for condemning Israel's airstrike on a hospital in

Gaza in November 2023, as politicians across the political spectrum accused them of "blood libel" and anti-Semitism—only for Israel to subsequently strike or bomb every remaining hospital in Gaza. Consider every headline that attributes information on Israeli terror attacks on Gaza to the "Hamas-run" Health Ministry. This is how credibility is assigned within an imperialist world order that unquestioningly privileges abusers over their victims.

The "attack" component of DARVO is just as stark in this situation as the "deny" component. Within days of October 7, Florida Governor Ron DeSantis, then running for president, declared that the United States can't accept Palestinian refugees, including children, because they're all "anti-Semitic."[26] Congressman Ryan Zinke introduced a bill to expel Palestinian Americans from the United States.[27] Congressman Brian Mast said there are "very few innocent Palestinian civilians."[28] Congressman Josh Gottheimer, ostensibly a liberal Democrat, sweepingly referred to Muslim Americans as "guilty."[29] Indeed, across the political divide, no matter how polarized the fabric of our political system, US politicians overwhelmingly align in their servile deference to Israel. The universal, unflinching refrain remains that Israel is defending itself, that Israel is the victim: "The way 'reverse victim [and] offender' works most often is to literally just say, 'To think negatively of me is unfair,'" Bedera told me, pointing to how criticism of Israel and dissent to US funding of the Israeli military are punished and broadly characterized as anti-Semitic. In October 2023 Tlaib, the only Palestinian American member of Congress, became one of just a handful of Congress members who have ever been censured in US history for her use of the decades-old slogan advocating Palestinian liberation, "From the river to the sea." Those very words dreaming of freedom are ostensibly violent—Israeli bombs are not.

The Zionist movement has subsisted on narratives of Israel's victimhood with tremendous success, which stands out to Bedera, because when actual abuse victims invoke their victimhood, they are heavily scrutinized and often further punished. Israel's campaign of endless, self-proclaimed victimhood has been effective for Zionists "as a group with a lot of power," in stark contrast with the lived reality of most victims.

Core to the construction of Israel's self-victimization narratives is rape-related atrocity propaganda that relies on racist, Western stereotypes and tropes about Muslim and Arab men. More than ever since October 7, Western media has propelled narratives of alleged mass, coordinated rapes perpetrated by Hamas against Israeli women. For merely pointing out the violence and war crimes—including widespread sexual abuse—that Israel has perpetrated against Palestinians, in December 2023, Democratic Rep. Pramila Jayapal faced vile smears accusing her of condoning sexual assault.

These were Jayapal's comments: "I think we always talk about the impact of war on women in particular. . . . I've condemned what Hamas has done. I've condemned the actions absolutely—the rape, of course," she said before shifting the conversation back to Israel and accusations that it has not been complying with international humanitarian law. "Morally, I think we cannot say that one war crime deserves another. That is not what international humanitarian law says."[30]

None of this is about supporting sexual violence victims. Anyone motivated by seeking justice for survivors would acknowledge how Israel's very existence creates the sharply unequal power dynamics that lead to sexual violence committed by Israelis against Palestinians with total impunity.

"Part of why I think that this is effective," Bedera said of Israel's strategy of self-victimization, "is because Israel, supposedly the woman, the victim, isn't defending themselves—it's the US arming Israel; the US then, in that metaphor, can step in as the man, the white knight intervening with arms." As for why atrocities perpetrated by Israel don't seem to matter to the US government: "Everyone knows or loves a rapist," she said. Pointing to the United States and Israel's decades-old, close relationship, she explained, "When it's someone you know and love, you're unlikely to see them as one; they're someone you want to take the side of." And, of course, the core language of DARVO is deeply familiar to US audiences: Violence and perceptions of aggressors and victims are inextricably and fundamentally racialized in the United States. Israel's racist language about Palestinians, including Prime Minister Benjamin Netanyahu smearing Palestinians as "children of darkness" and "barbarians" in 2023,[31] is "intended for an American audience," Bedera told me.

In the United States, the "fact that we have such a large military" similarly emerges from the language of victimhood, Bedera argues, "from language that we need to protect ourselves, we are the victims" of other countries—often countries the United States has colonized.

But credulity can only be stretched so far. Without end, for well over two years now, the world has watched what is perhaps the world's first televised genocide: Palestinian parents holding the remains of their children in plastic bags; entire bloodlines wiped out; the corpses of emaciated, starved children; children and dialysis victims burned alive in tents; families desperately trying to dig up their loved ones, buried alive under rubble, with nothing but their hands. Israel, we know, is responsible for making Gaza home to the most child amputees per capita in all the world.

All of *that* is Israel's so-called "right to defend itself."

The right to defend itself is inextricably bound to the right to exist. In the colonial imagination, only those in power hold that right. In the colonial imagination, state violence—violence in service of their ability to hold power—is *not* violence. In the colonial imagination, only revolutionary violence—violence that resists and challenges state oppression, as well as nonviolent protest or slogans like "free Palestine"—is recognized as a form of violence.

2

THE RIGHT TO PROPAGANDA

I say to the women's rights organizations, to the human rights organizations, you've heard of the rape of Israeli women, horrible atrocities, sexual mutilation? Where the hell are you?

—ISRAELI PRIME MINISTER BENJAMIN NETANYAHU

This iteration of Israel's genocide against Palestine is strikingly unique in one crucial respect: Since 2023, and for several years before that, it has been livestreamed on all our phones. This has been a genocide in which social media users I follow might post at noon only to be pronounced dead—murdered in an airstrike, massacred while waiting in line for flour—within hours. The brutality and utter inhumanity of this extermination campaign are undeniable, unmissable.

Writer Mary Turfah wrote in 2025:

> Initially the problem was thought to be a lack of awareness. If people knew, really knew, what was happening, what Israel was doing, which is to say, if people trusted any of many Palestinian accounts from any day over the last many decades or, short of this (we had to be realistic), heard the right testimony from a distraught non-Arab-appearing doctor (considering foreign journalists had been barred entry into Gaza), or watched the

> right video (taken from an expansive collection rich in its diversity) of Israeli soldiers savoring in their brutality, or of Israeli government officials underlining in biblical speech the absolute necessity of showing no mercy or squeamishness regarding the task at hand (total extermination), surely then something would switch. Or shift. Or give. Something.[1]

That didn't happen. She continued:

> Sometime after the shift or switch did not come, and before the come-to, people started writing things like, "what happens in Gaza won't stay in Gaza," often to try to shake the apparently unmoved. The boomerang effect: fascism always comes home. It's true that Gaza is a laboratory, and that Israel treats its enemies—within and without Palestine—like lab mice. It experiments with torture techniques on prisoners, trials biological weapons and security technologies over agricultural fields and residential neighborhoods, engineers new ways to make body and earth break. It is true that the environmental toll of Israel's genocide will not respect borders. What is equally true is that I shouldn't need to make Palestinians about anything else, to recognize that there is something very, very wrong, not about where we're headed, but about where we are. Who is it for, I've wondered, the "after they're done with them, they'll come for you"? Who looks at a Palestinian child and needs to hear that theirs could be next? Those for whom children are not enough.

But perhaps worse than turning a blind eye, supporters of the Zionist project turned an alert one—to anyone who offered even the mildest criticism of genocide. It was these voices, Zionists reasoned, that were violent—not bombs dropped on tents in Gaza, not ten Palestinian children a day who lost one or both legs to Israeli attacks. The violent ones, we're told, are the human rights activists and the few politicians who utter the words "free Palestine."

Propaganda and narrative control are tactics of violence. Abusers wield their disparate power and access to credibility and material resources to control public access to information, control what can and can't be said, and deny their victims the same agency. Through this vicious cycle, victims remain dehumanized and abusers can continue to justify their violence with impunity.

On June 24, 2025, New York City voters in the Democratic mayoral primary decisively chose pro-Palestine, Democratic Socialist state Assemblymember Zohran Mamdani—a thirty-three-year-old Muslim man—to be their next mayor.

Mamdani's campaign galvanized a generation of voters that had been slipping away from the Democratic Party's grasp. This time, voters aged eighteen to twenty-four constituted the election's largest voting bloc, whereas in the previous primary election in 2021, that was voters aged sixty to sixty-four. Mamdani appeared to build a broad coalition that the rest of his party had long seemed incapable of courting—likely owing to his platform of commonsense economic solutions, including a rent freeze, universal childcare, free buses, a $30 per hour minimum wage, and affordable, government-subsidized grocery stores. Unlike his chief opponent, Andrew Cuomo, a serially accused sexual predator and legal counsel to the Israeli war criminal Benjamin Netanyahu, Mamdani wasn't backed by billionaires or towering figures of the Democratic establishment like former President Bill Clinton—also a serially accused sexual predator.

But perhaps the most exciting part of Mamdani's victory was the sharp rebuke it issued to the chief strategies deployed by his rabidly Zionist, Islamophobic opponents. Those strategies relied heavily on smearing Mamdani as anti-Semitic for his record of activism against Israel's genocide. Cuomo's opposition ads frequently featured edited photos of Mamdani that thickened his beard[2] or depicted him clad in supposedly scary, ethnic garb to play up his Muslim identity and cater to the worst instincts of Zionist and Islamophobic voters.

Nevertheless, Mamdani defeated Cuomo by a resounding twelve points. Just four years earlier, when now-disgraced Mayor Eric Adams won the primary by about half a percentage point, he was lauded as the future of the Democratic Party.

Despite this, Mamdani struggled to secure endorsements from his own party leaders.

About two years into this iteration of Israel's genocide, Mamdani's success seemed to offer some cause for hope. Since 2023—but really for much longer—it's been impossible to track the number of public figures who have been fired, sanctioned, or censured for even mild criticism of Israel (or, in some cases, mere acknowledgment of the plight of Palestinians), due to the influence of pro-Israel lobbying groups. The words "never forget," regarding the Holocaust inflicted on the Jewish people by Nazi Germany in the 1940s, are seared into our collective consciousness—yet genocide denial to cover for Israel's crimes against humanity targeting Palestinians has become so pervasive that to even acknowledge Israel's genocide, to even hold the same position as every global humanitarian agency in the world, can be called anti-Semitic.

But after years of weaponizing and consequently hollowing out bad-faith accusations of anti-Semitism, Mamdani's victory showed that these accusations no longer hold the weight that they once did. His historic win served as, if not a referendum on, then at the very least a significant challenge to the political and cultural hegemony of Zionism and the rot of Islamophobia in US politics.

Yet, rather than reflect on the spectacular failure of their propaganda machine, Mamdani's Zionist opponents, including leaders of his own party, got to work wielding his victory to further validate their worldview—a worldview that frames Zionism as a marginalized, endangered ideology, and critics of Israel as towering, abusive oppressors. In the immediate aftermath of Mamdani's victory, prominent Zionist voices like the militant organization Betar began issuing warnings for Jewish residents to flee New York City, insisting that no Jewish residents could be safe if their Muslim neighbor became mayor.[3] All of this functioned as pure racism—ironically reinvigorating mass hate campaigns against *Muslim* communities—while being grossly couched in the language of victimhood, in the typical playbook of abusers.

At particular issue were Mamdani's very reasonable comments in June 2025, initially declining to condemn the slogan "globalize the Intifada," which celebrates global resistance to Israel's decades-long colonization and genocide of Palestine. And while "globalize the Intifada" is a perfectly reasonable thing to say, Mamdani did not say it. Instead, he'd said:

> I think what's difficult also is that the very word has been used by the Holocaust Museum when translating the Warsaw ghetto uprising into Arabic because it's a word that means struggle. And as a Muslim man who grew up post-9/11, I'm all too familiar in the way in which Arabic words can be twisted, can be distorted, can be used to justify any kind of meaning. And I think that's where it leaves me with a sense that what we need to do is focus on keeping Jewish New Yorkers safe. And the question of the permissibility of language is something that I haven't ventured into.[4]

Slogans of liberation like "free Palestine" or "globalize the Intifada" are framed by Zionists as calls for genocide against all Jewish people. But in what reality are words more dangerous or more genocidal than an actual genocide? These are words coming from those denied power, those who are fighting simply for their right to live. By contrast, lines like "Israel has a right to defend itself" reify the dominant power structures. The words "Israel has a right to defend itself" precede and then justify endless death, endless war crimes, endless suffering. But we're told instead that only "free Palestine" is scary and bad—because only this slogan challenges power and abuse, while the other maintains the status quo of normalized, colonial violence.

Meanwhile, through a continuous torrent of libel, then-Mayor Eric Adams sweepingly, baselessly called Mamdani an "anti-Semite" and supporter of Hamas. But Senator Kirsten Gillibrand of New York, whose top campaign contributors include the American Israel Public Affairs Committee, swiftly took the cake for deranged, self-victimizing responses to Mamdani's win. In a six-minute-long rant on a local radio station, Gillibrand baselessly accused Mamdani of supporting terrorism and a global "jihad" against Jewish people.[5] At one point, you could hear in her voice that she was on the verge of crying. This was a familiar dynamic. All too often, we have seen white women's tears wielded to demonize supposedly bestial, dangerous men of color. The oppressor's tears are meant to denote their victimhood—and their victimhood then justifies their abusive behaviors in the same breath. Gillibrand is a white woman who engaged in vile, racist attacks on Mamdani, but attempted to conceal this by framing *him* as the oppressor by nature of his identity and opposition to a supremacist status quo.

Mamdani, his Zionist critics declared, wanted to kill all Jewish people. He had said earlier in 2025 that, in accordance with international law, should Netanyahu set foot in New York City, he would support the Israeli prime minister being arrested for his range of crimes against humanity, which include facilitating genocide, mass starvation, and a campaign of indiscriminate rape and sexual violence against Palestinians. Mamdani's Zionist critics latched onto that reasonable and just campaign promise to arrest Netanyahu and claimed that Mamdani had threatened to arrest all Jewish people in New York City. Author Jill Kargman referred to Mamdani's victory as "a spiritual Kristallnacht,"[6] a line that so trivializes the Holocaust as to amount to Holocaust denialism.

All of these smears were appalling but not shocking. If anything, it was predictable. In 2023, I wrote the article "'Israel Has a Right to Defend Itself' and the Language of Domestic Violence" in the leftist publication *Prism*.[7] There's perhaps no greater example of an imperialist oppressor's co-optation of victimhood to justify perpetrating violence than the Zionist project of Israel writ large. We encounter this both in the sphere of American politics—a hostile environment set with death trap after death trap, landmine after landmine, to ensnare anyone who engages in the mildest criticism of Israel in career-ending, bad-faith anti-Semitism accusations—and in occupied Palestine, where even wishing to be free from the violence and oppression of settler colonialism is construed as genocidal, and grounds for Israel's so-called "self-defense."

■ ■ ■

If Democratic Party leaders didn't loathe their own base, with the rise of Mamdani's political star in 2025, they would have seen before them a golden opportunity. In recent years, the party has persistently struggled to appeal to anyone beyond neoconservative leaders like Liz Cheney and a handful of geriatric cable news viewers who worship the status quo but ultimately find President Trump to be a little mean. Too bad Democratic leaders very much *do* loathe their base. And so, they preferred to smear that base as a mob of "terrorist" sympathizers, rather than reflect on why someone like Mamdani—a bold critic of capitalism and critic of the wildly unpopular foreign regime committing genocide—excites people while the party's neoliberal, Zionist leaders have struggled to crack more than a few dozen viewers on digital livestreams.

I sometimes find myself haunted by the sincerity and forcefulness of Senator Gillibrand's racism as she accused Mamdani of being a "jihadist" determined to exterminate all Jewish people, simply for declining to condemn a slogan about Palestinian resistance and freedom. Of course, Gillibrand's comments were perhaps the most distinctly appalling, but the throughline between her words and the words of all the other Democratic politicians who implicitly or explicitly smeared Mamdani was the same. They presented

Mamdani as an Islamophobic caricature of hatefulness and violent fantasies against Jewish people, and, by proxy, pro-genocide politicians labeled his voters as anti-Semitic "terrorist" supporters. Together, Mamdani and his base are the oppressors. That framing then distracts from who the real oppressors are in this dynamic: Israel, and the US politicians who would rather sponsor Israel's genocide than fund resources for their own American constituents.

The Democratic Party's immediate reaction to Mamdani's victory also demonstrated its shameless willingness to shift goalposts when a candidate is Muslim, or a socialist, or critical of Israel. "Vote blue no matter who" applies only to candidates who back Israel's genocide to the hilt and choose austerity and trending, viral TikTok dances over redistributive policies. Over and over, we encounter the same: Leftists must vote for establishment Democratic candidates or shoulder the blame for Republican authoritarianism, while centrists have no obligation to do the same for leftists.

Such is the nature of the Democratic Party machine: flattening insurgent, people-power-led, leftist movements; framing their demands for basic dignity as patently absurd; and rooting out these movements in favor of the party's chosen mouthpieces of centrism and incrementalism. Half a decade prior to Mamdani's candidacy, we watched the party flatten Bernie Sanders' momentous presidential campaign, pressuring all remaining presidential candidates to bow out in favor of Joe Biden. That same summer, former President Barack Obama took the same approach to quash the fomenting of an NBA players' strike for racial justice, convincing the athletes to instead opt for symbolic jerseys emblazoned with the language of social justice rather than material demands.

And, speaking of moving goalposts: Consider the absurd, frankly outlandish standards Mamdani is held to, like the repeated, bad-faith questions about different oppressors' right to exist, like Israel and billionaires. I have made clear what I think of Israel's so-called "right to exist," and should make clear that, like Mamdani, I also reject the notion that billionaires have this same inalienable right, as their existence relies on massive wealth inequality. Mamdani, it must be noted, stood alone in receiving questions this hostile on the campaign trail. By contrast, Cuomo has a history of bizarre, overtly anti-Semitic comments,[8] while just days before the Democratic primary in June 2025, Adams publicly partied with the proudly anti-Semitic Twitch streamer Sneako.[9] Yet, because both Cuomo and Adams unconditionally support Israel, neither was questioned on his anti-Semitism; Cuomo, certainly, wasn't questioned on his status as legal counsel defending a foreign regime's war crimes.

To this day, I remain struck by the viral, wildly racist imagery of a pro-Mamdani flyer in New York City that was covered in a sticker that read "Believe Israeli women."[10] We know that sexual violence is an indelible feature of Israel's occupation of Palestine, yet, with stomach-churning success, Israel has pushed the baseless narrative that Palestinians are systematically sexually abusing Israelis, relying on racist stereotypes about Arab men to achieve this. The sticker in question was meant to smear Mamdani as a rape apologist at best and rapist at worst. But it speaks volumes about the sincerity of Zionists' concerns about sexual violence that this is how they treated a man with no allegations of sexual misconduct, all while embracing Cuomo, a man with at least thirteen such allegations.[11]

This slogan—"Believe Israeli women"—on its face conveys a willingness to broadly believe survivors. It's rare that survivors of sexual violence are near-universally believed. But to be clear, that's not at all what's happening here. "Believe Israeli women" is akin to pinkwashing. Like pinkwashing, the slogan selectively and performatively elevates a marginalized class—survivors—solely to advance a nefarious goal: the justification of genocide, the advancement of a racist narrative that depicts Arab men as innately violent, subhuman rapists. "Israeli women" are singled out by gender to obscure their status as colonizer, to conceal their disparate power and privilege, to position them—and by proxy, position Israelis as a whole—as victims, and Palestinians and Arabs as the abusers. Zionist propaganda that depicts sexual violence as a designated objective of the October 7 attacks is unsubstantiated; by contrast, sexual violence perpetrated by Israeli settlers and soldiers against captive Palestinians is extensively documented.

Ignoring Cuomo's and Adams's demonstrated hostilities toward Jewish people, the Anti-Defamation League, a Zionist propaganda arm that has embraced actual Nazis like Elon Musk solely because Musk embraces Zionism, continues to push public credulity to new extremes. Following Mamdani's win, the ADL rapidly broadened what he was required to condemn, ranging from popular, worldwide slogans to random social media users who are mean to Israel online.[12] It should speak volumes that whereas Palestinians' oppressors are nuclear superpowers who have locked them in a concentration camp and dropped tens of thousands of tons of bombs on that concentration camp in the last two years alone, Israel's and Zionists' oppressors, per the ADL, are social media accounts.

At its core, this exposes the fundamental disparities between what Zionists present as Jewish feelings of unsafety and the material reality: Mamdani faced credible death threats[13] on the campaign trail and calls for his deportation from the president and sitting Congress members. That was the natural consequence of racist smears that align him with terrorism and frame him as an existential threat to white Americans' lives. Yet, in the Zionist imagination, physical, structural threats that people experience due to Zionism, Islamophobia, and white supremacy are immaterial in the face of what a select group of people supposedly *feel* and *imagine* about him. At the time, in 2025, I was especially struck by widely shared social media posts from a Zionist influencer who claimed to feel safer in Israel than in Vermont.[14] After instigating war with Iran earlier that summer, Israel became a war zone—if one "feels" safer in a war zone than in the state of Vermont, that speaks volumes about the realness of those feelings.

The Zionist weaponization of these select, paranoid perceptions of a Muslim man advocating for peace compounds with Zionism's broader self-victimization propaganda. But fundamentally, this propaganda comes from a place of deepening weakness. It is not a winning approach—it is a desperate one. Support for Israel in the United States, certainly among young people, is at the lowest it has ever been.[15] And Mamdani's victory itself, overcoming all the vile Zionist propaganda efforts against him, cements this shift. Mamdani and Muslim communities were subjected to shamelessly Islamophobic attacks from Republicans and neo-Nazis, but Democrats and liberal Zionists hurled many of the same obscene smears at Mamdani and his base for months. None of it worked. Zionist politicians can keep going, spend the rest of their lives trapped in their hideous, increasingly bygone worldview of bigotry and delusion, alienate entire generations of voters, if they'd like. But Mamdani's political rise makes clear that the rest of us have moved on, that the world is moving on, too.

■ ■ ■

In December 2023, *The New York Times* published a lengthy investigative report that made sweeping claims about systematic sexual assaults perpetrated by Hamas fighters against Israelis on October 7.[16] But extensive fact-checking from publications including *The Intercept*, *Mondoweiss*,[17] and *The Electronic Intifada*,[18] as well as one of the *Times* reporters' own comments about the questionable process behind their reporting,[19] thoroughly discredit these claims.

In 2025, I spoke with media critic and journalist Adam Johnson, who has reported extensively on how US media has played a vital role in manufacturing—or at least attempting to manufacture—public consent to the genocide in Gaza.[20] One of the most salient approaches to justifying the genocide has been rape atrocity propaganda invoking October 7, wielding the known and unknown events of that day as a vehicle to cater to the West's most deeply held, violently racist fantasies. Whether or not one agrees with the choice of taking hostages to facilitate exchanges for thousands of Palestinian hostages (all as Israel effectively holds every Palestinian who lives under occupation hostage), Johnson pointed out to me that Hamas' actions were "in pursuit of a strategic goal," not a senseless spree of raping and killing as you'll see depicted in Western media. Only dehumanizing, racist tropes about Arab men, and particularly Palestinian men, as well as Western media bias heavily favoring Israel as a perceived ally to the West, have allowed hysterical reporting about Hamas-perpetrated mass rapes and atrocities on October 7 to flourish.

In 2024, *The Intercept* published a lengthy report that detailed a range of serious holes in the *Times* reporting. The article also made this important point: "The question has never been whether individual acts of sexual assault may have occurred on October 7," as "rape is not uncommon in war."[21] Yet, pervasive media coverage of a weaponized rape campaign remains unsubstantiated and deeply rooted in racism—all while Palestinian victims of sexual abuse say coverage like this has yielded heightened violence against them in retaliation.

Just weeks after the report was published, the *Times* reporter herself spoke at length with an Israeli radio station about how her reporting was largely driven by her deep-seated, preconceived conviction that mass sexual violence unfolded on October 7. She interviewed hospitals, police officers, and victim services facilities across Israel, and remained convinced a mass rape rampage had transpired—even after all of these sources told her they'd received no such reports and seen no evidence of rape. Paradoxically, the lack of rape reports and claims only further convinced the reporter that such a mass rape campaign had transpired and was being buried as part of an overarching conspiracy. Her only evidence was her racist certainty, but that was enough, apparently, for the *Times*.

The *Times* report wound up hinging on the word of decisively pro-war Zionist Israeli voices who were also behind a range of other debunked claims, such as readily disproven lies about forty Israeli babies beheaded by Hamas, a pregnant woman whose fetus was cut out by Hamas fighters (no pregnant women were killed on October 7), and Hamas fighters who sexually assaulted an Israeli woman and cut off her breast. One of the sources claimed to have seen twin sisters raped and murdered by Hamas in a kibbutz. But *Mondoweiss*'s fact-checking found no such sisters lived in the kibbutz in question, and found the source's other claims—about stabbed babies, Arabic messages written on walls in blood, and other claims that amount to atrocity porn—were false, too. None of these tactics of propaganda are new. Throughout the 1990s and early 2000s, Israel routinely and baselessly accused the Palestinian political leader Yasser Arafat of "beheading Jewish babies," wielding these lies to justify further aggression and conquest.

Nonetheless, lies about a horrific, organized rape operation have taken hold across leading voices advocating for the genocide. "I say to the women's rights organizations, to the human rights organizations, you've heard of the rape of Israeli women, horrible atrocities, sexual mutilation? Where the hell are you?" Israeli Prime Minister Benjamin Netanyahu said in December 2023.[22]

About one year later in January 2025, the Israeli government itself blocked a request from UN sex crimes experts to probe alleged sexual violence perpetrated by Hamas during the October 7 attack. The Israeli newspaper *Haaretz* reported at the time that this was meant to allow Israel to avoid the same scrutiny being applied to widespread sexual violence perpetrated by Israeli forces against imprisoned Palestinians, which could lead to Israel—not Hamas—being added to the UN's sexual violence blacklist.[23]

None of this halted the hyper-salient media narratives that had already taken form.

From October 2023 to October 2024, Johnson found that all mentions of rape during the Israel–Palestine war on Sunday cable shows concerned claims about rape allegedly committed by Hamas, and none by Israel. Far-right, pro-war Israeli voices who are caught making extreme, debunked claims are still deemed credible sources and quoted in outlets like the *Times*. In the summer of 2025, Bari Weiss, the Zionist media executive who founded the right-wing *Free Press*, oversaw propaganda that denied the existence of starving Palestinian children by blaming the children's preexisting health conditions. Within months, she would be appointed editor-in-chief of CBS News. Meanwhile, the mere act of being Palestinian can be disqualifying for sources or even journalists, Johnson's research has also shown.

"Very early on [in Western media], we saw this war on terror framing of the West versus an ontologically evil force, and this fundamental premise that this is a noble, just war to eliminate Hamas," Johnson told me in 2025. Where Israel is often "framed as reluctantly killing people"—even as Israeli forces have likely killed hundreds of thousands of Palestinians within a few short years—by contrast, Hamas's actions on October 7 are framed as "a nihilist rampage, a spree of killing people just to kill people and no other reason, not for any strategic goals. So it follows, under that logic, that they would only do things to be maximally evil," such as a deliberate rampage of sexual assault.

In a 2025 essay in *The Baffler*, Anna Krauthamer highlights the indelible nature of race and its social construction in how we perceive rapist and victim, offering the history of slavery and ongoing reality of racialized mass incarceration in the United States as an example:

> As Black men continue to be disproportionately imprisoned every year, furthering the United States' ongoing carceral project, violence against Black women often fails to make itself visible. How racial hierarchy dictates the very terms of rape's social imaginaries—who we think does it and to whom we think it is done—plays out cruelly and consequentially in the entwined

> U.S. histories of enslavement and sexual violence. It makes visible how central race is to the history of rape and reveals the state as an unreliable guarantor of justice.[24]

Rape-related atrocity propaganda smearing Palestinians has several functions. In addition to manufacturing consent to genocide, it obscures Israel's well-documented role as a perpetrator of sexual violence against the men, women, and children they've colonized.

■ ■ ■

United States and Israeli relations are deeply rooted in the politics of relatability, in Western perceptions of Israel as a civilized beacon of light and hope in the uncivilized, dehumanized Middle East. Israel, in the Western imagination, is coded as white: a Western ally surrounded by uncivilized, barbaric, bestial Arab nations. The relatability between Israel and the West lies heavily in their perceptions of a shared, brown enemy. Israel's social media campaigns, barbaric in their attempts at cutesiness and epicness while the country simultaneously carries out a world-historic extermination campaign, make clear they know their audience.[25] The obsessive invocations of the supposed October 7 mass rape campaign show precisely how Israel caters to the confluence of notions of liberal feminism and the white supremacist instinct to protect white-coded women from uncivilized men of color. But Israel's utterly bizarre, childlike social media presence demonstrates a broader, overarching effort to appeal to the West and sanitize its deep-seated brutality.

In November 2023, within the span of a week—a week spent bombing universities, refugee camps, and the only hospital for cancer patients in Gaza—the Israeli state X (formerly known as Twitter) account tweeted at Taylor Swift not once but twice, first sharing an unsubstantiated story about one of Swift's security guards reportedly joining the Israeli occupation army, and again to plead with Swift to express support for Israeli hostages. The same Israeli social media account declined to prop up the voices of hostages' family members who were pleading for a ceasefire, as Israel continued to indiscriminately bomb and kill its own people.

As Israel's genocidal campaign rapidly escalated in the final months of 2023, the ethnostate simultaneously became more and more active on state social media accounts. Its online activities included harassing Palestinian American supermodel Gigi Hadid on Instagram, tagging her in a graphic photo ostensibly depicting murdered Israeli children; sassily "clapping back" at the UN Geneva X account for daring to implore Israel to abide by international law; cyberbullying peace activist Greta Thunberg by claiming that the materials in Hamas's rockets aren't sustainable and that the "victims of the Hamas massacre could have been your friends," all while polluting the world by incessantly bombing Gaza; sharing fan-art-like graphics that inexplicably equated Hamas with Voldemort; and forcing its way onto all of our social feeds (and even children's video games) through paid ads featuring graphic images and language about Gaza and Hamas. The language and imagery attached to the posts read as direct appeals to American and Western audiences.

"There's an element of impersonation going on," Dr. Marc Owen Jones, an associate professor at Hamad Bin Khalifa University whose research focuses on social media and disinformation in the Middle East, told me in 2023. Israel is "masquerading as a Gen Z [or] as a millennial" online as it engages in trolling behavior reminiscent of a 4chan or 8chan account. "The gotchas, the 'smackdowns,' the vulgarity to the whole thing. . . . It's as if [Israel has] got a marketing consultant that tells them, 'If we tweet like this, we'll get more engagement.'"

Susan Brewer, a professor emeritus of history at the University of Wisconsin–Stevens Point and author of *Why America Fights: Patriotism and War Propaganda from the Philippines to Iraq*, told me Israel's online activities reminded her of what we saw in the United

States at the onset of the Iraq War in the early 2000s: "a very deliberate campaign" in mass media—cable news, radio, ad campaigns—that "was made to look as though [the invasion of Iraq] was in response to the terrorist attacks of 9/11," she said. The United States created a propaganda campaign to address public doubt and push back on critics who questioned the US government's true motives to rush into its war on Iraq because "there were many doubters and critics, so there had to be a steady march of ratcheting up the need to do this," she said. Israeli state social media places a similar emphasis on the supposed necessity of its massacre of Palestinians, framing these murders as justified retaliation for October 7.

Wartime propaganda in mass media has historically followed many of the same patterns, Brewer said. The dehumanization of the supposed enemy is paramount, and nothing dehumanizes a population more than narratives about them butchering babies—an accusation levied by the United States against Arafat and Iraqi leader Saddam Hussein in the early 2000s, and, years later, by pro-Israel advocates against Hamas in 2023. Though the Israeli Occupation Forces eventually ceded that viral claims that Hamas had beheaded Israeli babies were unsubstantiated, the damage, as Israel well knew, was done.

Today, Israel's digital presence reflects the historical wartime propaganda playbook for a social media age. Social media presents a new medium for dissenting against war and combating the propaganda pushed by politicians and legacy media that didn't exist during the Iraq War or World War II—but it also opens up new avenues for manufacturing consent and disseminating propaganda. As Palestinians share their ongoing, devastating experiences with the world, Israel is visibly scrambling to respond in kind with its own digital campaigns. Posting aggressively, utilizing the shock factor and sensationalism, the Israeli account's tweets reflect the hysteria and intensity of radio hits and posters across the United States during the Cold War to combat "communism."

David Saranga, the director of the digital diplomacy bureau in Israel's Ministry of Foreign Affairs who oversees Israel's social media presence, told *Rolling Stone* in November 2023 that his team "is comprised of about 30 individuals, ranging from department heads to seasoned digital consultants, language managers, interns, and graphic designers." Saranga manages "more than 20 accounts in six languages" and estimates these accounts have "reached 2 billion people in the past month."[26] Saranga confirmed to *Rolling Stone* that appealing to the West is, indeed, his chief strategy: "We have put out more than 2,500 posts in the last month that have reached over a billion English speakers," he said. Through social media, Saranga explained, many users "finally understand the barbaric enemy we are fighting," referring to Palestinians. Propagandists know their audience: As Israel relies on Western nations for military aid and political validation, its social media posts cater to Western sympathy by mirroring our social consumption, by mimicking pop star accounts, by pandering to Swifties. "The demographic that they generally want to target, if you look at the paid ads they've done, is the West, 100 percent. That's where they know the power is, the demographic they have to appeal to in order to sustain the military funding that enables Israel," Jones told me. "They've lost the Middle East."

In 2013, the Associated Press reported that Israel hires college students specifically to defend its government and the occupation of Palestine on social media.[27] At the time, Netanyahu's office called the initiative "a groundbreaking project aimed at strengthening Israeli national diplomacy and adapting it to changes in information consumption." A spokesperson for Israel emphasized that social media activity is central to the regime's identity. In December 2022, when *Jewish Insider* first introduced Saranga to the world, he stressed social media's prominent role in Israeli diplomacy, telling the outlet that he instructs Israeli envoys to get active on all social platforms "to prepare for the future, in case something happens." He added that Israel had just joined TikTok at the time to reach Gen Z.[28] When Saranga was asked about the Israeli military's killing of Palestinian American journalist Shireen Abu Akleh and a sixteen-year-old Palestinian girl named Jana Zakarneh, both in 2022, he stressed the importance of social media "to put it all in the right context," explaining, "The right context is the fact that it's a war zone and there are terrorists there who are fighting with Israeli forces and are trying to penetrate Israel, to spread violence. It's our duty to protect our citizens."

Pro-Israel propaganda extends beyond the influx of online content being force-fed to social media users by Israeli state accounts. "The flip side of propaganda is censorship and shutting down debate and questions," Brewer told me. Dissent to the Iraq War, for example, was met with condemnation, loss of work, surveillance, state punishment. Since 2023, employers across all industries have declared their refusal to employ workers who protest Israel's genocide. Social media users and activists who shared content critical of Israel and supportive of Palestine on social media have reported being shadowbanned or having the reach of their content limited by social media companies. Some have accused Meta and other social platforms of arbitrarily removing pro-Palestine content for violating unspecified "community guidelines."

The punishment and diminishing of pro-Palestine voices offline and online, Jones told me, comes as Israel has continuously flooded social media timelines without end: "[For Israel], it's about muddying the waters—at some point, it becomes effective when people don't know what's true anymore," Jones said. Social media users "become skeptical of everything. They don't know what to believe. And that inevitably benefits the attacker, the aggressor."

In the United States, which is the top contributor of military aid to Israel, 66 percent of all voters—including 80 percent of Democrats, 56 percent of Republicans, and 57 percent of independents—supported a ceasefire by October 2023.[29] Referencing Israeli social media strategies, Brewer said, "If you feel that everyone's already convinced, you don't need to do this."

Sure, all world governments propagandize. But not all plead with Taylor Swift for a shout-out while bombing children's hospitals, all while simultaneously trying to feud with Swift's close friend Gigi Hadid—predictably accusing her of supporting "mass rape."

The ability to propagandize is withheld altogether from victimized entities. Palestinians are denied the right to share information. In digital spaces, they are dismissed as "spam" and "bots" when they ask for help. They are denied speaking slots on cable news, unless they condemn Hamas while Israel starves them. All too often, abusers deny their victims the right to construct their own narratives about their experiences. State propaganda in service of imperialist powers applies those same tactics on a structural level. Colonizers flood the zone with atrocity propaganda, depictions of their colonized victims as the aggressors, as baby killers, as rapists, as racialized caricatures of pure darkness, and themselves as the victims. And, as the victims, they must respond, resist, "defend" themselves by any means necessary—including genocide.

3

THE RIGHT TO RAPE

A failed state is now often a rape state.

—RANA JALEEL

In the spring of 2025, Zionist filmmakers rolled out the documentary *October 8*, a film that bills itself as a crushing portrayal of anti-Semitism in the United States since October 7, 2023. *October 8* premiered as hundreds of Palestinians were being murdered in Gaza by the day, as thousands starved, and as survivors were indiscriminately carted off into concentration camps rife with torture and sexual violence. But the real victims, we were told, were white Americans, safe and sound in their homes in the United States, made slightly uncomfortable by the sight of Palestinian flags and keffiyehs. The film was produced by billionaire Sheryl Sandberg, who notably helped oversee the social media giant Meta in 2016 as the company permitted pervasive disinformation and hate speech that fueled the genocide against Rohingya people in Myanmar. Since 2023, Sandberg has zeroed in on promoting Zionist propaganda smearing Palestinian men as rapists, spreading unsubstantiated but nevertheless pervasive mythologies about a supposed "mass rape campaign" by Hamas fighters on October 7. Before *October 8*, Sandberg produced the purposefully inflammatory, disinformation-ridden documentary *Screams Before Silence* about this topic in 2024.

Hillary Clinton, a frequent purveyor of rape-related atrocity propaganda against Palestinians, shared *Screams Before Silence* with her followers in 2024. Throughout her failed presidential campaign in 2024, Kamala Harris's central talking point to justify Israel's genocide was her repeated line about "horrific rapes" by Hamas, which she invoked at the presidential debate, in her Democratic National Convention speech, and in all public remarks about the genocide.

In *October 8*, several speakers incessantly hammer this line home. Dan Senor, a prominent Zionist author and podcaster, says at one point in the film, "It was October 8. . . . There was still fighting going on. Israel was still counting the numbers of the dead, and the mutilated and the raped and the kidnapped. And there's a protest against Israel in Times Square. Rather than the outrage being directed against those slaughtering the Jews, the outrage was being directed against the Jews for objecting to being slaughtered." By "objecting to being slaughtered," Senor is, of course, referring to dropping the equivalent of two nuclear bombs on Gaza—a 141-square-mile plot of land with a population that disproportionately comprises children under eighteen—within the span of less than a month in 2023. That detail is conspicuously excluded.

This incessant fixation on imagined mass rapes functions as a highly manipulative rhetorical tool: Anyone who questions the nonexistent evidence of a coordinated rape campaign by Palestinians against Israelis, or questions why anything should justify genocide, steps into the trap of appearing to be a misogynist and a rape apologist—especially when this propaganda is being peddled by female presidential candidates and corporate feminist CEOs who style themselves as advocates for women. In reality, anyone who selectively invokes sexual violence to push racist, false narratives about Palestinians, but never to address the years of systematic sexual violence against Palestinians by the occupying force that holds all power over them, very clearly isn't concerned with sexual violence.

In June 2024, *The New York Times* published a report on the brutal conditions at Israel's Sde Teiman prison, including testimony from survivors that Israeli officers had committed wide-ranging, horrific acts of sexual torture.[1] Later, leaked surveillance video from the prison broadcast showed Israeli soldiers appear to gang-rape a Palestinian man. When the video gained enough traction to yield surface-level consequences for those involved, Israelis launched a series of mass public demonstrations in defense of Israel's right to rape Palestinian detainees.[2] Rioters stormed a military base where the accused rapists were being held and demanded that they be freed and face no criminal charges. The rioters clashed with soldiers and infiltrated the base's gates, chanting their support for the rapists, who some Israeli politicians referred to as "heroes" and "heroic warriors."[3]

These horrors are only the tip of the iceberg.

The Carnegie Endowment for International Peace reports that more than one million Palestinians have been detained and held captive by Israel since 2023, often on unspecified "administrative charges."[4] Forty percent of all Palestinian men have been detained by Israel since 1967, and 70 percent of Palestinian families have at least one member imprisoned by Israel; 700 Palestinian children are detained by Israel every year, and Israel is the only country in the world that systematically and automatically tries children in military court.[5] Child sexual abuse is rampant in these dungeons, Defense for Children–Palestine has reported.[6] But you'll never encounter public outcry for the conditions that Palestinian hostages face, nor any recognition that they are, in fact, hostages at all, in the Western imagination.

Sde Teiman wasn't an isolated offense. In 2022, Palestinian journalist Wafa Ali Al-Udaini wrote an extensively reported feature on the horrific conditions that Palestinian women face in Israeli prisons. Al-Udaini noted that, at the time, Israel had arrested more than 16,000 Palestinian women since 1967, and pointed to extensive documentation of torture, sexual degradation, denial of family visits, solitary confinement, poor or nonexistent medical care, and lack of education.[7] One woman she interviewed recounted enduring "a living hell." That woman had been arrested at an Israeli checkpoint in 2015 for allegedly spying for Palestinian resistance groups and was sentenced to six years in prison despite a total dearth of evidence presented by Israel. "Being trapped in the draconian Israeli prison quickly overwhelms and ferociously devours our lives," she told Al-Udaini.

A different woman, who was pregnant when Israeli forces detained her and refused to provide essential prenatal care, gave birth in prison and said she was told by an Israeli guard, "You are a terrorist, and soon you will put a new terrorist into the world." This woman had a C-section while her hands and feet were handcuffed to the hospital bed. She said that her baby "left my womb, entered another tomb."

Israel killed Al-Udaini alongside her entire family on September 30, 2024.[8]

The Israeli military occupation is, itself, an extension and form of gender-based violence as it creates the sharply unequal power dynamics that lead to Israelis committing sexual violence against Palestinians with total impunity. The occupation and colonization broadly produce an innate, inescapable vulnerability to sexual violence for Palestinians, who are routinely terrorized, detained, and abused by Israeli forces as a feature of everyday life, from routine border checkpoints to frequent home invasions and body and strip searches. Since October 7, Israeli, American, and Western politicians as well as liberal feminists have zeroed in on unsubstantiated, racist lies about a mass rape campaign perpetrated by Palestinian men on October 7, both as implicit justification for the genocide, and to distract from the mass sexual violence perpetrated by Israel—which has only escalated since October 7, as Israeli soldiers across occupied Palestine retaliate for these unsubstantiated rape myths by punishing Palestinian women and girls.

Sexual violence is a feature of domination, and domination is the very goal of imperialism. Historically, sexual violence was—is—an indelible feature of colonization, enslavement, and war, a tool to flex and enforce power, to impress upon the victims, the colonized, their own powerlessness. In the United States, white women alleged that bestial Black or brown men had raped them to justify the full range of racial terror, from lynchings to territorial expansion to endless war, and with it, endless rape. In Vietnam in the 1970s, American soldiers systematically raped and sexually enslaved colonized women, a reality that remains both widely acknowledged and widely dismissed to this day. As sexual violence researcher Anna Krauthamer has written in *The Baffler*, during the Balkan wars of the 1990s, wartime sexual violence "was enormous in scale and notoriously brutal," to the extent that "the evidence of mass rape undermined, on a global scale, an earlier concept of rape as a private violation outside of the scope of international law." Consequently, "the scale and nature of these crimes made them legible not only as war crimes and human rights violations but as acts of genocide," she wrote.[9]

Like all wars before it, and like all genocidal campaigns of domination and violation in history, Israel's campaign in Gaza is deeply rooted in gender, humiliation, abuse. Across all cultures, today and throughout history, sexual and gender-based violence has always functioned as a tool of empire. The American institution of chattel slavery is inseparable from the United States' sweeping legacy of sexual violence to enforce colonial authority in the most brutal possible fashion, to punish, to reproduce slavery and create an infinite supply of exploitable slave labor. The Vietnam War saw the US military wield rape and sexual violence as a de facto weapon of war. Today, this brutal colonial pillaging is remembered in the form of crass jokes hypersexualizing and objectifying Asian women.

State sexual violence persists today in the United States, at home, as it always has, ravaging underclasses to violently enforce social and political hierarchy, and further victimizing those with the least power by designating them as threats—not unlike domestic abusers engaging in DARVO. In 2001, Sisters Inside, an Australian abolitionist group that advocates for incarcerated and formerly incarcerated women, first presented the term "state sexual assault."[10] They argued that the state itself is a perpetrator of sexual violence through policing, incarceration, and the physically invasive violence these institutions require. State sexual assault entails strip searches and cavity searches performed by state agents on incarcerated or arrested people; it is the enabling of pervasive sexual assault by police officers and prison guards, the general punitiveness and systemic denial of incarcerated people's bodily autonomy within carceral systems. Sisters Inside organizers who had been incarcerated themselves described how physical and sexual abuse from interpersonal partners and from agents of the state carry many of the same impacts and feel virtually indistinguishable from each other. State sexual assault encapsulates how sexual violence transcends interpersonal attacks alone, how the state itself is a purveyor of sexual violence, by creating the very conditions that allow interpersonal sexual violence to thrive.

In scholar Rana Jaleel's 2021 book, *The Work of Rape*, she writes, "A failed state is now often a rape state," articulating how Western powers identify barbaric, backward societies that urgently need to be liberated via imperialist violence.[11] Invasions of these "rape states," these societies that are systematically violent toward women and girls, are feminist victories in the Western, liberal imagination. If Gaza is a "rape state," if Hamas is coded as an army of rapists with no other purpose but rape, rape, rape, then of course its extermination, the extermination of all Palestinians, is warranted if not altogether feminist in the Western, liberal imagination. Who cares that this extermination campaign, itself, is a weaponized avenue for mass rape with impunity? Who cares that this extermination campaign becomes Israel's "right to rape"?

In early 2025, an Israeli prosecutor conceded there were no rape reports associated with October 7, contrary to continued Zionist propaganda about supposed "mass rapes" perpetrated by Hamas that day.[12] I don't pretend to know everything that happened on October 7, but that is immaterial: There is zero evidence of any sort of coordinated "mass rape" campaign whatsoever; all of the narratives that serve to sweepingly frame Palestinian men as rapists rely entirely on racist narratives about barbaric, foreign men who need to be colonized. Following this admission from the Israeli prosecutor, I wondered, at the time, whether any amount of evidence to the contrary of the "mass rape" propaganda would ever halt it. I couldn't imagine that would be the case, as it's all the Zionist movement has to sustain itself at this point. So, I started talking with victim advocates and legal experts about the enduring salience of this particular talking point. Even more insidious than justification for genocide, one victim advocate told me, the "mass rape" lies have catalyzed heightened gender-based violence—against Palestinian men, women, and children—perpetrated by Israeli settlers and soldiers across occupied Palestine.

Kifaya Khraim worked as the international advocacy coordinator at the Women's Centre for Legal Aid and Counseling (WCLAC), based in Ramallah in the West Bank, when I spoke with her in January 2025. Khraim had spent the previous two years taking the reports of Palestinian women and girls who say they were subjected to sexual assault, sexual torture, and rape by Israeli soldiers. The incidents of violence across all occupied Palestinian land increased dramatically after October 7, in tandem with Israel's genocide against Palestinians in Gaza. From dozens of women across the West Bank, Gaza, and Jerusalem, many of the stories are the same, Khraim told me: women arrested without charges and held under administrative detention, forced to strip, strip-searched, repeatedly beaten on their genitals, photographed naked, threatened with or sometimes subjected to rape. The violations occur at detainment centers, or at checkpoints, as a condition of their ability to move from one place to another, or, increasingly often, when soldiers invade their homes in the middle of the night. Some of the women Khraim heard from said that while in Israeli jails, they came to fear falling asleep, as they believed they'd be raped or assaulted—they were certainly threatened with as much.

Khraim and her colleagues ultimately deduced that there is a "higher directive" for soldiers to violate and threaten Palestinian women and girls, since the acts of sexual violence are so uniform across different places and different Israeli army units. The Israeli soldiers understand and exploit the fact that cultural stigma will prevent many of their victims from coming forward, she said. Soldiers harass their victims for months on end afterward with phone calls to their homes, threatening to further harm them or ruin their lives if they report their experiences to human rights organizations or authorities. "Women are terrified to talk about what happened to them, and we have to give them so many assurances to convince them to talk to us," Khraim said. "We've interviewed over thirty women prisoners; they all say the same thing: They were tortured, they were denied food, they were denied sanitary pads, they were assaulted and beaten in front of each other, all to humiliate them."

It's not just the genocide in Gaza that's escalated acts of sexual violence from Israeli soldiers across Palestine. Israelis are further emboldened by Western media coverage of the genocide—particularly extensive coverage alleging a systematic "mass rape" campaign perpetrated by Palestinian men against Israelis on October 7—prompting worsened sexual violence against Palestinians across the occupation as collective punishment. "Soldiers feel more compelled to retaliate and take revenge, because that's what they believe happened," Khraim told me. They even feel comfortable "posting [their abuses] to social media, talking about it so freely and casually," because Western media reports about sexual atrocities by Hamas have further convinced so much of the world that Palestinians are "human animals." Israeli Defense Minister Yoav Gallant characterized Palestinians as such, verbatim, in October 2023.[13]

To be unequivocally clear, to this day, allegations of a coordinated campaign of sexual violence by Hamas are unsubstantiated; rather, they draw on overtly racist stereotypes that not only implicitly offer grounds for genocide, but justify the occupation more broadly. Such has always been a tactic of colonizing powers: painting colonized men as barbaric rapists who must be punished, tamed, and controlled, and can't be entrusted with freedom and self-determination. Yazan Zahzah, a member of the Palestinian Feminist Collective, told me that throughout history, we see Black and brown men broadly smeared as rapists who pose an innate threat to white or Western women, justifying lynchings and executions by colonizing forces and white supremacists. All the West hears about from mainstream media, Zahzah said, is "trigger words" about "how Islam oppresses women, about sexual violence, how Israel is trying to defeat this." Israel is construed as Western, civilized, the perpetual victim of scary, incurably bloodthirsty brown people.

We encounter a similar tradition in the United States, where the social construction of race and caricatures of certain groups as more threatening have long justified brutal state violence. Historically, Black and brown men have also been reduced to bestial, hypersexualized caricatures to justify an array of state violence and deny self-determination. In the United States, the state has condoned extrajudicial, white supremacist violence in the form of lynchings; in the famous case of Emmett Till, a Black child was tortured and killed by a horde of white men in response to a white woman's claim that the child had whistled at her. At least 4,743 lynchings occurred in the United States from 1882 to 1968, though the NAACP estimates this to be an undercount.[14] The perpetrators justified this racial terror and brutality by framing their victims as an innate and immediate physical threat—primarily to white women and girls—just by existing. Today, a rising tide of xenophobia demonizing immigrant men from Latin American countries, and, in particular, portraying them as rapists and distinct threats to white, American women, has yielded a range of sweeping, anti-immigrant policies. Take, for instance, the Laken Riley Act, a law that invokes the murder of a twenty-two-year-old white woman by an undocumented man to sweepingly dismantle the civil rights of both citizens and noncitizens across the United States—all while placing certain classes of survivors, like immigrant survivors, at greater risk.

Liberal Zionist voices, Zahzah told me, will often express some level of sympathy for Palestinians in Gaza, but, as we saw from Kamala Harris, temper that sympathy with references to an atrocious campaign of sexual violence against Israelis by Hamas. In effect, "they're trying to equalize who holds power in the situation," Zahzah said, and to suggest that the most overt parts of Israel's genocide are wrong, but that Palestinians are still innately violent and need to be occupied. The liberal Zionist movement is rife with such tensions and hypocrisies, Zahzah argued, pointing to how liberal US Zionists often advocate for reproductive rights, but ignore the horrific reproductive injustice across Gaza amid the genocide—including total decimation of the health care system, C-sections without anesthesia, and surging rates of miscarriage and maternal and infant mortality and infections.[15] "We don't see that regarded as a form of gender-based violence," Zahzah said.

For all of Western media outlets' reports about "mass rapes" perpetrated by Hamas, consider the dearth of coverage of sexual violence perpetrated by Israelis against Palestinians. When Palestinian sexual abuse victims never see their stories or experiences come to light, they don't see any point in coming forward and are distrustful of human rights groups that seek their testimonies. "This makes it harder for us to collect data and testimonies," Khraim told me, "because we're asked, 'What are you using it for? We don't see it anywhere in media.'" Consequently, lack of data and testimony make it more difficult to hold Israel accountable or push for transparency, protections, and change.

The testimonies that Khraim *has* been able to document have been chilling: One woman was arrested after soldiers asked her why she was wearing green; she was taken to a police station, stripped naked, and beaten on her genitals while cameras recorded. Many women, Khraim said, are arrested and jailed solely due to social media posts deemed dangerous or anti-Israel, or being insufficiently deferential to Israeli soldiers. Months before October 2023, in July of that year, Israeli soldiers raided a home in Hebron, threatened five women, including a seventeen-year-old girl, with large dogs and guns, and forced them to get naked. Khraim says she's tracked at least thirty similar cases of Israeli home invasions in which women and girls have been forced to undress on threat of violence and detainment.

Palestinian women are particularly vulnerable to sexual violence at checkpoints, where Khraim and WCLAC have documented at least five such incidents. In one case, an Israeli soldier exposed himself to a woman and made her touch his genitals. Women are unable to report this violence at checkpoints because they fear retaliation, which could result in them being unable to pass in the future and go to work or school. The consequences can be long term and devastating. Girls and young women are unable to go to school if they fear invasive body searches at these checkpoints. One of Khraim's colleagues at WCLAC has said they've tracked cases of girls married off at young ages by their families "out of fear," so they can move elsewhere and be safe from sexual abuse by the Israeli occupation. Eva Tabbasam, director of Gender Action for Peace and Security, warned *Middle East Eye* in December 2024 that while sexual violence committed by Israeli forces is by no means new, it's "increasing at an alarming rate."[16]

Sexual violence against Palestinians is not just institutionalized but openly glorified across Israeli culture: In August 2024, large crowds of Israeli citizens led violent riots in protest when Israeli guards were arrested for raping and sexually torturing Palestinian captives. Rioters broke the rapists out of jail and asserted their perceived right as Israelis to rape Palestinians. The lead suspect among those guards, a man named Meir Ben-Shitrit, is now a prominent Israeli television personality.[17] As sexual violence researcher Anna Krauthamer wrote in *The Baffler* in 2025:

> Once Israel's cynical mobilization of rape to advance its decimation of Palestinians began, it seemed impossible to halt. These allegations reaffirmed existing narratives of the civilized versus the uncivilized, compounded by the need to protect (Israeli) women. This is partly why reports in the *New York Times* [in 2024] of Israelis systematically raping male Palestinian prisoners in Sde Teiman and elsewhere received so much less attention: they did not cohere with the established worldview of who rape's perpetrators and victims are. . . .
>
> The United States and Israel position these same people as patriarchal would-be rapists to justify the expansion of the settler project. Perversely, Israelis are the ones actually raping Palestinians—and using fictive rapes to justify their genocidal project.[18]

ProPublica reported in January 2025 that there is significant evidence the US State Department has been made aware of horrific abuses—including sexual abuses—perpetrated by Israeli soldiers against incarcerated Palestinians.[19] In the report, children recount torture and brutal mistreatment; one fifteen-year-old boy from the West Bank said he was tortured and raped in the Israeli detention facility Al-Mascobiyya. Child sexual abuse within Israeli prisons is rampant and well documented: In 2014, the Palestinian Prisoners Club reported that Israeli forces arrested at least 600 Palestinian children in Jerusalem and subjected nearly half to sexual violence.[20] Global humanitarian organizations Save the Children, Human Rights Watch, and Defense for Children International have offered corroborating reports of prevalent child sexual abuse in Israeli jails through the years. In December 2023, when Defense for Children International informed the United States that Israeli forces had raped a thirteen-year-old Palestinian boy in an Israeli jail and the United States brought this to Israel's attention, Israel shut down the organization's office the following day and declared it "a terrorist entity." All six prominent Palestinian NGOs were designated as terrorist organizations by the Israeli government in 2021 for reporting on Israel's abuses.

The goal is the total silencing of reports of sexual abuse perpetrated by Israel.

■ ■ ■

As previously mentioned, in March 2025, the United Nations Independent International Commission of Inquiry on the Occupied Palestinian Territory published a fifty-page report on "genocidal acts" committed by Israeli forces and settlers against Palestinians.[21] This was the fifth report by the commission documenting atrocities committed by Israel since October 2023, and it focused on gender-based violence against Palestinians, including rape, sexual torture, and targeted attacks on their ability to safely give birth, or give birth at all. "Sexual and gender-based violence—which has risen in frequency and severity—is being perpetrated across the Occupied Palestinian Territory as a strategy of war for Israel to dominate and destroy the Palestinian people," the commission's press release presenting the report stated. "Forms of sexual and gender-based violence including rape" are "committed either under explicit orders or with implicit encouragement by Israel's top civilian and military leadership."

Drawing on both witness and survivor testimony, as well as social media posts from Israeli soldiers and settlers themselves, the report details pervasive sexual violence against Palestinian men, women, and children. These behaviors have escalated since October 7, 2023, but the report stresses that "sexual and gender-based violence is by no means a new element of the Israeli occupation," under which Palestinians are routinely subjected to strip and body searches at checkpoints, or rampant sexual abuse and beatings on their genitals in jails and detainment camps. Palestinians of all ages and genders report frequently being arrested without charge. In detainment camps, male survivors recount sexual torture and being stripped naked and repeatedly, severely beaten, especially on their genitals. Their humiliation, they said, appeared to be the goal. Women and girls recount being similarly, routinely subjected to strip searches, forced nudity, beatings on their genitals, and threats or completed acts of sexual assault while detained.

"I've always said Arabs [female pronouns used] are the biggest sluts out there," an Israeli soldier says in one video posted to social media and reviewed by the commission. This video is one of many in which Israeli soldiers record themselves looting Palestinians' homes and stealing and wearing women's lingerie. In other videos, not just in Gaza, Israeli settlers record themselves kidnapping Palestinians, making them strip, humiliating them, and, in at least one, forcing them to eat straw and animal food.

The commission's report states that Israel has "deliberately" imposed "measures intended to prevent births" and concludes that Israel is guilty of "the crime against humanity of extermination." Chris Sidoti, an international human rights lawyer for more than four decades who serves on the commission and co-wrote the report, spoke with me about their findings. Sidoti cited the case of Israeli forces directly targeting and destroying a fertility clinic in Gaza that stored at least 4,000 embryos.[22] The commission determined that Gaza's 540,000 women and girls of reproductive age have been left without access to sexual and reproductive health care; consequently, rates of deadly infections, miscarriage, and maternal and infant mortality have surged since October 2023. C-sections in Gaza hospitals are performed without anesthesia and adequate medical supplies. Many women give birth in tents; those who give birth in overrun hospitals are almost immediately discharged.

Describing her struggles with starvation and no access to health care, one new mother who gave birth during the genocide told the commission, "It was a lot for me, it was a lot for women. It's more than a human can bear."

The commission spoke with Palestinians who prepared for their births by watching online videos, because they knew they wouldn't be able to receive care. In some cases, pregnant or postpartum women are killed by Israeli forces: "One of my patients had just given birth to twins when her apartment was attacked" in August 2024, a lactation consultant in Gaza told the commission. "The attack happened while the father was at a local government office to register the birth. The woman and her newborns were killed instantly in the attack," he said, and "there was no militant in sight."

The report continues, "Entire families in Gaza have been killed together in their homes in unprecedented numbers," further referencing previous UN reporting that "95% of women were killed together with at least one child." The UN similarly found that women and girls have been forced to "[minimize] their need to go to the toilet . . . by avoiding eating and drinking." They fear infections and diseases from unhygienic conditions, and also for their safety while "having to use the toilet in close quarters with men."

One woman told the commission, "We cannot afford pads. If we have money, the priority is to bring food for the family to survive rather [than] getting pads for something that is temporary." The commission interviewed another woman at Gaza's Al-Shifa Hospital who suffered from infections from lack of clean water. These infections only worsened at the hospital, she said, as "there was garbage spread everywhere inside the hospital, as it was not safe to take the garbage outside" because Israeli forces routinely attack hospitals or shoot at anyone who steps outside.

"The legal definition of genocide is very technical and not always the same as popular understanding," Sidoti told me. Israel has "created conditions that make continuing life impossible, impaired birth—even destroying fertility clinics—and impaired the reproductive capacity of women, also men, through deliberate injuries to their genitals." Gender-based violence has always been a feature of Israeli forces' occupation of Palestine, Sidoti said:

> It can only be described as systematic, at this point, and it's far more intense now than what was experienced [before October 7]. We came to the conclusion [that acts of gender-based violence] are a specific policy, a method of war on the part of the Israeli military. It can't be said these are isolated incidents by rogue soldiers—it really is part and parcel of the way Israeli forces are conducting this fighting. That is very disturbing.

Since October 7, violent "body searches," sometimes as a pretext for rape, have all escalated, Sidoti said. "Clearly, security isn't the concern, when [Palestinian] detainees are kept naked for several days, sitting on the ground in the cold during winter, or in prison cells, still not allowed to wear clothes—it really is about humiliation and inflicting pain, denying Palestinians, as a people, all dignity."

Palestinians of all genders and ages are subjected to this treatment when detained by Israel. But Sidoti told me that most testimonies about sexual violence in Israeli-run camps were from men and boys: "We have testimony from men and boys who suffered grievous physical harm to their genitals and anus, from mistreatment and sexual violence from Israelis—we believe this is far more widespread than previously known."

"When you look at Israeli soldiers, you wonder how they could be ordinary human beings after this, to come out of a genocidal campaign of this brutality, to their families, kids, communities," Sidoti told me. "You wonder what Israeli society will look like after this, how much more domestic violence and sexual assault there may be."

“There is no escape from the conclusion that Israel has employed sexual and gender-based violence against Palestinians to terrorize them and perpetuate a system of oppression that undermines their right to self-determination,” Navi Pillay, chair of the commission, said in a statement about the report in March 2025.[23]

Amnesty International’s senior adviser on gender, conflict, and international justice, Lauren Aarons, said of the report shortly after its release: “These damning findings are another clear illustration of the devastating impact of Israel’s genocide in Gaza and its use of gender-based violence to oppress . . . Palestinians of all genders, especially in Israeli detention centers.” She continued, “No discussion of human rights is possible without tackling Israel’s decades-long impunity for its violations against Palestinians. The world must act to ensure justice is a reality for all Palestinians and to restore some faith in international law for all.”

The silence from US political leaders on the commission’s findings about genocidal, gender-based violence by Israel against Palestinians was deafening. To Sidoti, who has extensively documented human rights violations by Israel over his decades-long career, this silence was unsurprising. He’s grown accustomed to American media conspicuously not covering systematic sexual violence against Palestinians, he told me. “There’s never much US response to anything we [the commission] produce. But so far as Israel–Palestine is concerned, the US is irrelevant. US political leaders’ views just don’t matter—they’ve established their position, which is one-sided and uncompromising. They don’t have credibility because of that.”

Nevertheless, Sidoti is ultimately “confident” that Israel will face accountability, even if not immediately: “We’ve already seen the International Criminal Court issue arrest warrants for Netanyahu and other Israeli officials, and the court said that’s just the start. There’s no statute of limitations on international atrocities. I hope they know they’ll be pursued to the grave.”

In its imperialist arrogance, the United States rarely considers its positioning and reputation in the rest of the world. The United States' unwavering devotion to Zionism through every Israeli atrocity has robbed it of any moral credibility. At the same time, to Sidoti's point, the world doesn't revolve around American feck-lessness. Other nations and global advocates for human rights will step up to fill the void of the United States' moral leadership and pursue justice and accountability against Israel. The tide is turning, and most of the world sees Israel for exactly what it is: a nation born in genocide and actively perpetrating it for all the world to see.

When we spoke in January 2025, Palestinian victim advocate Kifaya Khraim told me that, where it was once almost impossible to collect testimony from Palestinian sexual assault survivors victimized by Israelis, that is starting to change. Stigma and terror silencing Palestinian victims remains pervasive, she said, but over the course of 2024, she was able to collect testimony from more and more Palestinian victims. Many have remained reluctant, as they haven't seen their testimonies yield change or media coverage. But as more women come forward, more are emboldened to join them.

Any amount of media coverage of their experiences—coverage contradicting Zionist, rape-related atrocity propaganda—can be galvanizing, Khraim said.

4

THE RIGHT TO HAVE A FAMILY

At its core, Zionism denies Palestinians the right to exist, thrive, and have autonomy over their bodies. . . . This racist ideology is incompatible with reproductive justice. Zionism is a contradiction to reproductive justice.

—ARC-SOUTHEAST

What good is a movement that demands "freedom to parent" but looks away when families of color are systematically denied the ability to raise their children in safety and dignity?

—JA'LONI AMOR OWENS

Mahmoud Khalil, a Palestinian student organizer and US green card holder, was held in a US Immigration and Customs Enforcement (ICE) detention center in Louisiana during the birth of his son in the spring of 2025. Months earlier, as a recent graduate of Columbia University, he was arrested and detained by ICE agents who didn't have a warrant for his arrest, all in front of his then-seven-months-pregnant wife, Noor Abdalla. For more than three months, Khalil, who was born in a refugee camp after his family was displaced by Israel, was held in the ICE facility more than 1,000 miles away from where his wife gave birth. His crime? Protesting Israel's genocide against his people. His own university colluded with the Trump administration to make his imprisonment possible.

In an op-ed days after his son's birth, Khalil wrote his "first words" to his newborn son: "During your first moments, I buried my face in my arms and kept my voice low so that the 70 other men sleeping in this concrete room would not see my cloudy eyes or hear my voice catch," he wrote. "Why do faceless politicians have the power to strip human beings of their divine moments?" Further:

> In Palestine, this pain is part of daily life. Babies are born every day without their fathers—not because their fathers chose to leave, but because they are taken by war, by bombs, by prison cells and by the cold machinery of occupation. The grief your mother and I feel is but one drop in a sea of sorrow that Palestinian families have drowned in for generations.[1]

Khalil continued to shine light on the loss and dehumanization of all the fathers around him at the ICE facility. "I have come to recognize the look in the eyes of every father in this detention center. I sit here contemplating the immensity of your birth and wonder how many more firsts will be sacrificed to the whims of the US government," he wrote, further raising the hypocrisy of how "the same politicians who preach 'family values' are the ones tearing families apart."

Halfway across the world in Gaza, by April 2025, the humanitarian agency UNICEF counted 39,000 new orphans.[2] The violence against children and families has been so extreme that aid organizations like Doctors Without Borders were forced to coin the new term WCNSF (Wounded Child, No Surviving Family).[3] In the spring of 2024, UNRWA estimated thirty-seven mothers in Gaza were killed by Israeli forces every day.[4] This genocide functioned as a fundamental war on not just children and families, but the very right of a population to give birth, to reproduce, to exist with any continuity or dignity. Imperialist violence is, at its core, gender-based violence, reproductive violence; imperialist powers reflect abusive partners exerting control over their victims' bodies and reproduction.

Israeli officials consistently frame Palestinians as an existential threat to Jews' very existence as a people; the slogans "from the river to the sea, Palestine will be free" and "globalize the Intifada," Zionists say, are calls for the total extermination of Jewish people. But this performance of victimhood then becomes a pretext for the total extermination of Palestinians, routing family lines, sniping at pregnant women trying to go to hospitals, imposing starvation conditions, conditions of unthinkable barbarity, to render it impossible to give birth safely, to give birth at all.

In October 2023, the women of color–led reproductive justice organization ARC-Southeast shared a letter of solidarity with Palestinians, characterizing the Israeli occupation as settler colonialism and denouncing how Israel's policies (including 2013 reports that Israel oversaw forced sterilizations targeting Ethiopian Jews) have denied Palestinians bodily autonomy.[5] The letter drew dozens of signatories, including Indigenous Women Rising, the National Network of Abortion Funds, and the Feminist Women's Health Center. It states:

> At its core, Zionism denies Palestinians the right to exist, thrive, and have autonomy over their bodies, something that impacts Palestinians of all genders and ages. This racist ideology is incompatible with reproductive justice because we know firmly that settler colonialism denies the core tenets of RJ. Zionism is a contradiction to reproductive justice.

Ja'Loni Amor Owens, an attorney and reproductive justice advocate based in the South, wrote in an op-ed that Khalil's case presents not just an immigrant justice and free speech issue, but a reproductive justice issue. Owens called on reproductive rights and justice organizations in the United States to mobilize in support of Khalil and against family separation:

> If reproductive justice organizations can't fight the disappearing of a Palestinian father as his wife prepares to give birth, what is their commitment to reproductive freedom worth? What good is a movement that demands "freedom to parent" but looks away when families of color are systematically denied the ability to raise their children in safety and dignity?[6]

■ ■ ■

The right to have a family has never existed for everyone. White supremacy and imperialism have often obstructed or denied this right altogether for colonized and marginalized classes. US wars that swept the Global South birthed an entire international adoption-industrial complex in countries like Vietnam and Cambodia, enriching US companies that traded in connecting upper classes with orphaned or relinquished babies of color, severed from their families by imperialist violence.[7]

Or consider the extensive histories of kidnapped Indigenous children in the United States, stolen from their families and communities, violently forced to forfeit all cultural identity. Indigenous, Black, and Latine communities were explicitly targeted by the US eugenics movement, which peaked in the 1920s; and today, forced sterilizations through varying legal loopholes have persisted in both prisons and immigrant detainment centers.[8] The legacy of the US family policing system persists to this day, as certain communities face heightened policing for behaviors during pregnancy or early parenting, and white supremacy continues to shape who is and isn't perceived by the state as a responsible, fit parent.

To have a family on your own terms is a human right. But under imperialism, it is rendered a privilege—a privilege denied to the colonized, certainly, as colonizers hold a vested interest in controlling and even ending their victims' reproduction.

By the summer of 2024, research published by *The Lancet* journal estimated that nearly 186,000 Palestinians in Gaza had been killed within less than a year. Women and children constituted 70 percent of the casualties. And pregnant people, menstruating people, and particularly children suffered disproportionately from the dearth of available reproductive care. Within a few short months, the miscarriage rate in Gaza had soared 300 percent, CARE International told me for my reporting in early 2024;[9] later that year, the organization Medical Aid for Palestinians reported the maternal mortality rate had increased 20 percent since October 2023, and the infant mortality rate had increased 15 percent.[10]

Emergency C-sections were routinely performed without anesthesia, sometimes when pregnant women were on the brink of death, as doctors tried to save their premature babies. These C-sections have resulted in excruciating pain and deadly infections. Hospitals and the medical system are entirely overwhelmed, directly targeted by the Israeli military, and devastated by Israel's total blockade, which refuses to permit basic sanitation supplies, painkillers, or fuel, even to save the lives of premature babies who rely on incubators to breathe. And since October 2023, more and more babies have been born premature or unhealthy.

In April 2024, I spoke with UNICEF officer Tess Ingram, who had visited Gaza's only standing maternity hospital, Emirati, in January of that year, and again right before I spoke with her.[11] The number of sick and unhealthy babies and pregnant women had increased substantially from January, she said, explaining, "It's because, at this point, a pregnant woman in April has spent more of their pregnancy during the war than a pregnant woman in January. What we're seeing is the real, obvious impact of war, deprivation, trauma on pregnancies; we're seeing many more preterm, weak, sick babies." Ingram told me, "It's an absolutely nightmarish place to be a pregnant woman, beyond words, and it is a hellish environment to be born into."

A few days before Ingram spoke with me, she'd visited a woman who was pregnant when an Israeli attack forced her to flee her refugee camp in Khan Yunis, Gaza. After running for her life from tanks that were shooting at her and other refugees, she made it to Emirati, where she learned she'd miscarried. Her condition required her to have an emergency C-section and subjected her to "an incredible amount of pain." Another woman, Wala, was forty years old and gave birth to her seventh child just seventy-two hours before Ingram spoke with her. Wala, who wasn't able to get her blood pressure medication for months by then, birthed a preterm baby who weighed just 4.4 pounds. Displaced in a refugee camp in southern Gaza, she slept in a tent without a mattress and shared two cans of food each day between herself and her seven children.

Another pregnant woman in Gaza named Mashael was buried alongside her husband under rubble for several days after an Israeli airstrike, Ingram recounted. While Mashael was under the rubble, her baby stopped moving; a month later, while waiting for medical care at the hospital, she learned she'd miscarried. "She was heartbroken that this, her second pregnancy, had ended, but said she felt it was best 'a baby isn't born into this nightmare,'" Ingram said.

Around the same time that I spoke with UNICEF, CARE International shared with me the testimonies of other postpartum women in Gaza, including one mother who described sheltering in "a small house" with twenty-five people, with no sanitary products for women, which caused "diseases and epidemics [to spread] everywhere." She further wrote that "some of my friends had their babies without anesthesia, even when having cesareans," an account corroborated by several other humanitarian workers I spoke with at the Palestinian Family Planning and Protection Association (PFPPA) and World Health Organization.

Samah Shamali, a former lecturer at the Islamic University of Gaza, shared a Facebook post in early 2024 detailing horrific stories of pregnancy and birth in Gaza.[12] Shamali described a pregnant woman who was repeatedly run over by an Israeli tank until her fetus came out. She described another woman who went into early labor and had to walk ten hours; when she gave birth, the woman's newborn premature twins died from a lack of available oxygen supply at the hospital. One woman who went into labor where she was sheltering was unable to call an ambulance because of a blackout imposed by Israel and was forced to walk to the hospital.

Ammal Awadallah, executive director of PFPPA, told me she'd heard similar stories from patients and health care providers on the ground in Gaza—in fact, these experiences "are more common than not."[13] Awadallah spoke with one woman who was discharged from a hospital immediately after having a C-section with nowhere to go, since she and her husband feared going to an overcrowded shelter, especially since her cesarean wounds made her vulnerable to infection. "[They] were calling out into the streets for anyone to take them in," Awadallah said. She also learned about a woman who "didn't know she was pregnant and didn't find out until miscarriage, for which she was relieved, and [she] felt she was fortunate" to not give birth during the war. "Everybody now is displaced, and there's no food or clothing, so that even after the newborns are born, they don't have anything to dress them in. There's nothing—no medicine, no food, shelter."

In the summer of 2024, three health care workers at PFPPA recounted what they'd witnessed serving pregnant patients and infants in Gaza over the previous year: One woman in Khan Yunis in Gaza went into labor in the middle of the night, which is when the shelling and attacks from Israeli forces become more intense. While trying to reach the hospital, the ambulance she was riding in was attacked by Israeli forces. She and her fetus both died.

One of the health care workers I spoke with in October 2024 was killed by an Israeli airstrike months later, in January 2025. Israel's targeting of hospitals and health care workers can only be understood as an act of genocide; Israel is not just murdering civilians but making an example of anyone who deigns to help save Palestinian lives. Doctors who have survived Israeli detainment have recounted torture and brutal, inhumane conditions in prison camps, but many others don't survive.

In the summer of 2024, PFPPA also shared the story of one of their own health care workers, Wafa Abu Hasheish, who miscarried while fleeing a bombing. "I was able to find a doctor only after reaching Rafah, who confirmed I was miscarrying. I didn't even realize I was pregnant," the mother of three said in a post on social media. In the same post, Awadallah wrote, "A woman who conceived at the start of these hostilities will now be giving birth. . . . This will be a lost generation in Gaza, a generation born in genocide."[14]

Due to limited resources, Awadallah told me that, as time passed, more and more C-sections and births were "being performed without basic medical supplies or anesthesia, and without any postnatal care." As a result, "women are being dangerously exposed to infections." She said she'd "seen women with C-sections developing infections that spread right up to their chest."

Toward the end of 2024, a group of doctors published an article in *The Lancet* journal pondering whether there will be any "future for newborns in Gaza," warning that Israeli forces are deliberately targeting maternity hospitals as well as blockading medical supplies like maternity kits.[15] "Our colleagues in Gaza . . . who face the horrors of this large-scale violence daily, report an unprecedented rise in maternal deaths, miscarriages, and stillbirths. The malnutrition that many pregnant women endure only exacerbates these outcomes," the article states. "The prevention of births within Gaza is not merely collateral damage—it is a violation of international law, a grim reminder of the structural violence imposed on this population."

Even if Palestinian women in Gaza were able to birth live babies, often enough their trauma was just beginning: "When people talk about PTSD, it doesn't apply to Gaza, because it's never 'post.' It's a situation of continuous trauma," Awadallah said. "Previously, Gaza was an open prison, but now it's fully closed. It's a cage."

When I spoke with James Elder, the UNICEF officer who routinely works in war zones, toward the end of 2024, shortly after he returned from his fourth visit to Gaza that year, he told me that on that trip, he'd visited hospitals in the middle region of Gaza. He called Israel's genocidal campaign "the most horrific war on children" he's witnessed yet: "That isn't just a headline. That's the reality."

"It gets worse every single time I return," he said. He recalled hospital floors "absolutely packed with elderly and children" and the pervasive "smell of burning flesh, almost everywhere I went." At Al-Aqsa Hospital, he befriended a six-year-old child named Hamid who suffered from "fourth-degree burns so severe he had no skin left." Prior to meeting the child, Elder said he hadn't even heard of "fourth-degree burns"—the horrors in Gaza are at a scale so intense, he said, that he has often been forced to learn new medical terms.

"I personally have held the hands of children taking their last final gasps with no family alive, all their family killed in the same attack, unable to comfort them during their final agonizing breaths," Dr. Tanya Haj-Hassan, who served in Gaza, told reporters in the summer of 2024 at a press conference outside the Democratic National Convention,[16] which refused to platform a single Palestinian speaker. "The children who are fortunate enough to survive their injuries are discharged into a Russian roulette of 100 different ways that they could be killed by the conditions manufactured by the Israeli military campaign—another bombing, starvation, dehydration, disease."

At the same press conference, Dr. Feroze Sidhwa said he "saw children's heads smashed to pieces by the bullets that we paid for, not once, not twice, but quite literally every single day." Dr. Ahmad Yousaf said he witnessed an endless stream of children "carried in pieces by their loved ones" to overrun hospitals; he recounted trying to treat a woman who was twenty weeks pregnant when she was brought to the hospital with "burns that covered over 70 percent of her surface area" after a bomb dropped on her while she was in her own home. The burns were "a death sentence in an environment" lacking even basic medical supplies. Dr. Thaer Ahmad recounted treating a five-year-old girl whose leg had been "nearly blown off" by a bomb. The same bomb killed two of her younger siblings and "her father lost both of his legs." They were attacked while sheltering in what they were told was a "safe humanitarian area."

This is precisely the world that Israel has come to normalize for pregnant people and their loved ones across Gaza: a world in which words—like "safe" or "humanitarian"—are void of meaning, and the ability to give birth without bombs raining down above one's head is regarded as a privilege.

About 100 physicians who served in Gaza wrote a letter to President Biden in the fall of 2024, one year into the genocide. "With only marginal exceptions, every single person in Gaza is sick, injured, or both," they wrote. "We worry that unknown thousands have already died from the lethal combination of malnutrition and disease, and tens of thousands more will die in the coming months, especially with the onset of the winter rains in Gaza. Most of them will be young children."[17]

In the spring of 2025, the United Nations Independent International Commission of Inquiry on the Occupied Palestinian Territory's report on genocidal acts of gender-based violence committed by Israel stated that Israel has "systematically destroyed sexual and reproductive healthcare facilities across Gaza" and "deliberately" imposed "measures intended to prevent births." In its first pages, the report details a pervasive belief across Israeli government and society that "Palestinians in Gaza are complicit, despite age, gender, or civilian status, and should be exterminated."[18]

My conversations and correspondence with these health care workers and humanitarian organizations coincided with the ongoing devastation of reproductive rights across the United States—the fallout of the 2022 *Dobbs v. Jackson Women's Health Organization* ruling that had killed *Roe v. Wade*, gutting the legal right to abortion.

In January 2024, I spoke with a group of feminists who protested at Joe Biden and Kamala Harris's "Restore *Roe*" campaign rally. The event marked the fifty-first anniversary of the ruling, as the then-Democratic ticket attempted to underscore the stakes of reelecting Donald Trump—who, of course, brags about being the one to kill *Roe*. One of the Palestinian American protesters I spoke with said that, as security guards forcibly removed her for disrupting Biden's speech, the president called her a Trump supporter.

She wasn't, of course.

But that was the context in which the Biden administration, waist-deep in facilitating a genocide of world-historic brutality, perceived and labeled her: an extension of Trump, an oppressor.

Reporting on the crisis of reproductive injustice in the United States and the Gaza genocide's endless consequences for pregnant people and children, I have felt myself pulled in a hundred different directions. Death, violence, and hypocrisy have long pervaded almost every aspect of American life. But that particular moment amid the 2024 campaign trail felt like an especially jarring referendum on prevailing narratives about the universal sanctity of human life, as dueling realities often struck at the same time, evoking wildly different reactions from political leaders. To the Democratic establishment, all things were black and white, colored solely by the threat of Trump's reelection. A Democratic presidential administration's outsized role in facilitating genocide and unthinkable reproductive violence abroad was immaterial, under this logic—American women were dying, American women were being tortured, and Biden, we were told, would save them. Those who opposed Biden for any reason consequently aided Trump; those who opposed Biden were the oppressor—a clear-cut reversal of victim and offender.

We encounter this strategic deployment of DARVO at every level of politics. In New York City, Zohran Mamdani's protests of Israel's genocide similarly resulted in his opponents framing him as the abuser in 2025, ignoring if not bolstering his opponents' racist, abusive attacks on him by smearing *him* as the "anti-Semitic" oppressor. Within the first week after Mamdani's victory, then–Democratic House Minority Leader Hakeem Jeffries immediately proclaimed that he wasn't ready to endorse Mamdani, and alluded to imagined, offensive comments and behaviors from Mamdani toward Jewish communities, which Jeffries didn't bother to specify. Rep. Eric Swalwell of California said he disagreed with Mamdani's comments about Jewish people, without specifying what those comments were. Of course, Mamdani's only on-record comments on Jewish communities advocate for equality, peace, and safety, so it's concerning that Swalwell would "disagree" with any of that. Rep. Dan Goldman similarly said he couldn't endorse Mamdani until the Democratic nominee, who is notably not a trained trauma therapist, could sufficiently soothe and heal every Jewish New Yorker's worst fears about him, even if those fears were racist and untethered to reality.

Those who hold power—the abuser, the institution, the state—will perform powerlessness time and again so as to consolidate that power and justify further, reactionary violence. The Biden administration insisted it was powerless to follow international law, to meet the resounding and popular demands for peace, for an end to the bottomless fount of bombs and weapons and money for a foreign apartheid regime committing genocide. Instead, we were told, the people who held all power were the voters, the Palestinian activists whose families were being exterminated, the student protesters putting their bodies on the line against police brutality and a rising tide of fascist, state violence—these parties were to blame for giving us Trump.

Domestic abuse and state violence in service of an imperialist agenda are inseparable from each other here; performative victimhood becomes the very vehicle through which others are victimized.

■ ■ ■

In December 2024, a masked figure shot and killed UnitedHealthcare CEO Brian Thompson outside a Manhattan hotel building in the early hours of the morning. Security footage of the incident became a widely shared meme within hours of being made public. A Facebook post from UnitedHealthcare announcing Thompson's death was quickly inundated with tens of thousands of laugh reactions compared with a few hundred sad reactions. Eventually, the company turned off comments on the post, as its comment section became saturated with users sharing personal stories of being denied insurance claims by United—it was either stories of that nature, or a continuous stream of jokes.

"My empathy is out of network for this one," some social media users wrote. Others: "Pre-authorization for our condolences required [smiling face with sunglasses emoji]"; "Thoughts and prior authorizations." Another wrote, "You're laughing? a wealthy CEO who profited off of the health concerns and often worst moments of millions of peoples lives got shot point blank in broad daylight and they can't find the suspect bc too many people wanted him dead to narrow it down and you're laughing?"[19]

One comment on a 2023 LinkedIn post by Thompson told the CEO, "UnitedHealth Group is failing my mother by not providing her the basic care. . . . You continue to delay any decision making and authorizations which is compromising her health even more." Another reply said, "Hey Brian, I just spent an hour on the phone battling to get general information for my wife who has stage 4 cancer. She's a 45-year-old mother of 4. I'd love to share my experience with you." And another: "You are doing a great job cutting your costs. Not having a single anesthesiologist in the entire state of Montana is a great policy to save you money."

Private insurers reject about one in seven claims from individuals seeking coverage. United, specifically, manages to lead the pack, rejecting a third of claims.[20] Reporting from 2023 revealed that the company had recently started using an AI model to dehumanize its clients and determine which sick people to deny coverage to; United continued to use the model even after finding it had a staggering 90 percent inaccuracy rate.[21]

Before his death, Thompson's posts on LinkedIn were often rife with heartbreaking stories and pleas from people with family members battling terminal conditions who were still being denied coverage. People lose loved ones every day to the health insurance industry; it's not just guns—policy kills, too.

When Rep. Rashida Tlaib spoke at the Democratic Socialists of America Convention in August 2025, she told delegates, "The violence against our people doesn't have to come in the form of a bomb or a gun. The systems and structures around us kill our neighbors. It's the same effect."

Few publicly mourned Thompson, but certainly not everyone celebrated his death. In response to memes and more lighthearted takes, some political leaders occupying the tired role of civility police reminded social media users that compassion was in order because Thompson "had a family." Democratic Rep. Ro Khanna called Thompson's murder "horrific," adding, "I mean, this is a father we're talking about—of two children, and . . . there is no justification for violence."[22]

"[Thompson] has two children that are going to grow up without their father," Senator John Fetterman said of Thompson in December 2024. He called those who engaged in online jokes, and celebrations, and those who used Thompson's death to highlight the innate violence of the US health care system, "vile."[23]

Fetterman's invocation of Thompson's children, amid his own endless support for Israel's genocide in Gaza, says it all, really. Israel leads the world in child murder. But Fetterman's sympathy has at no point extended to these children, to their families, to the children across Gaza and occupied Palestine left without limbs, left without parents, thanks to Israel. Fetterman extends his sympathy, instead, hypothetically, to the surviving children of an American mercenary of death and suffering.

Civility is paramount, we are so often told by the very people who are killing us with their policies. This chastising reminded me of all the horrific state violence imposed by abortion bans on women and pregnant people, who are then told that protesting outside Supreme Court justices' homes or confronting anti-abortion elected officials in public is the *real* violence, the *real* threat to safety.[24] In the neoliberal political imagination, "abortion" remains a concept—not a material issue, not a health care service that can determine someone's entire future, even whether they live or die. In a similar vein, under the logic of neoliberalism, slowly—but sometimes quickly—choking the life out of someone by denying their access to health care is just a concept, a policy disagreement.

Of course, "having a family," as we are endlessly reminded that Thompson did, is not accepted as valid currency for everyone—not Palestinians whose entire family lines have been wiped out amid the genocide in Gaza, nor Palestinians and pro-Palestine dissidents in the United States who are being targeted and detained by the state for their advocacy against genocide. And "having a family" certainly isn't accepted as valid currency by health insurance companies denying coverage to people with life-threatening ailments. Between 35,327 and 44,789 adults aged eighteen to forty-nine die every year in the United States due to lack of health insurance; a death toll including children and people fifty years or older would likely be much higher.[25] Also in the United States, 60 percent of personal bankruptcies are driven by medical debt—a term that should not even exist.[26]

In the year leading up to Thompson's death, the same US politicians who insisted that "violence is never the answer" and chastised those who justified Thompson's death had spent each day funding, arming, and manufacturing consent for Israel's genocidal campaign in Gaza.

Large swaths of US politicians are decidedly bought and owned by the very health insurance industry that systematically kills sick and poor Americans. Their hollow condemnations were void of even passing reflection, and they made no effort whatsoever to interrogate the frustrations and trauma that might drive individuals to commit violence. They made no effort to understand violence perpetrated by those without any other power as a *response* to violence—a *response* to state violence.

Senator Elizabeth Warren of Massachusetts offered some consideration to why Thompson's death garnered little public sympathy. "The visceral response from people across this country who feel cheated, ripped off, and threatened by the vile practices of their insurance companies should be a warning to everyone in the health care system," she said. "Violence is never the answer, but people can be pushed only so far. This is a warning that if you push people hard enough, they lose faith in the ability of their government to make change, lose faith in the ability of the people who are providing the health care to make change, and start to take matters into their own hands in ways that will ultimately be a threat to everyone."[27]

She continued, "The number of people I personally hear from, both in my official capacity and as somebody who stops and talks to people in the grocery store about how hard it is to get medical care that people have paid their insurance companies for over and over and over, is a reminder that this system is just broken."

The system is not just "broken." It is killing people—at least tens of thousands, likely more—and certainly shrinking the lifespans of large swaths of the population along lines of class. Thompson's killer killed one; Thompson's killer used a gun, whereas politicians use policy, and health insurance companies use bureaucracy and the slow, agonizing torture of forcing the poor and sick to become poorer and sicker, to the distress of their loved ones, until their dying breath.

Within a week of Thompson's death, under distinctly peculiar circumstances, law enforcement identified and apprehended Luigi Mangione, an Italian American graduate of the University of Pennsylvania, for Thompson's murder. Mangione faced four federal charges: murder through the use of a firearm, two counts of stalking, and a firearms offense. These charges qualified him for the death penalty. Manifestos and social media posts that authorities attributed to Mangione excoriate the United States' for-profit health care system, while Mangione's loved ones recounted his debilitating struggles with a painful, chronic back condition.

A Reddit account that appears to have been linked with Mangione advised fellow Redditors suffering from chronic, debilitating back pain on how to navigate the cruel intricacies of the for-profit medical system: "Tell them you are 'unable to work' / do your job."[28]

"We live in a capitalist society," he said. "I've found that the medical industry responds to these keywords far more urgently than you describing unbearable pain and how it's impacting your quality of life."

Mangione allegedly shot Thompson in Manhattan during the same week that a New York jury acquitted Daniel Penny, the twenty-six-year-old white man who strangled Jordan Neely, a homeless, mentally ill Black man, to death in 2023 for the crime of exposing his fellow subway riders to his suffering. Penny has since been embraced as a hero by the dominant, right-wing political party, whereas Mangione faced a terrorism charge—and, notably, there are no charges yet for the health insurance CEOs whose policies kill untold numbers of Americans each year.

On May 1, 2023, different videos of Neely's murder show that, inside a subway car, he shouted about being hungry and thirsty, and that he didn't care if he died or went to jail. Penny then came up from behind Neely and put him in a choke hold. Penny sustained the choke hold for about six minutes, even when it was clear that Neely was dying, and even when the subway doors opened and passengers could safely exit. "He's dying. Let him go!" an unseen bystander said in the background of one video captured by another passenger.

Still, Penny's attorneys and the bloodthirsty, right-wing culture warriors who have since valorized him have insisted Penny is a hero and an upstanding citizen who kept his fellow subway riders safe. Penny's attorneys even argued that it wasn't the choke hold that killed Neely, but Neely's schizophrenia medication.[29]

Additional medical records reviewed during the trial showed that after being hospitalized for depression at fourteen, Neely was diagnosed with schizophrenia. He told a doctor in 2017 that his experiences with homelessness and poverty, including being forced to "dig through the garbage" for food, caused him to feel so hopeless he considered suicide. Shortly after Neely's death, reporting came to light about his yearslong struggles in the foster care system, how he often gave his own money earned from street dancing to fellow foster kids for food and clothes, and how he struggled after losing his mother, whose boyfriend was convicted of murdering her.[30]

Neely had a family. He had experienced the loss of his family. Conveniently enough, Penny's supporters never acknowledge these aspects of Neely's life.

A legal defense fund for Penny raised nearly $2 million within days of his arrest in 2023, with significant boosts from prominent right-wingers like Florida Governor Ron DeSantis and Kid Rock.[31]

For years now, the right has frequently invoked the events leading up to Neely's death and his public mental breakdown to inflame panics about public safety, all while deliberately ignoring the cruel policies and conditions that condemned Neely to homelessness and starvation. Yet, if anything, Penny's acquittal presents a public safety threat by suggesting that you can kill anyone for daring to suffer in front of you in a public place. The classist and white supremacist systems of violence that dehumanized Jordan Neely, that empowered a white man to murder him in broad daylight with total impunity, present the greatest possible threat to our collective safety.

Mangione allegedly killed a man who, one could easily argue, killed or helped kill untold numbers of people; as I write this, Mangione is sitting in jail and staring down the death penalty. Penny, who killed a poor Black man, now has a lucrative consultant job. Within days of being acquitted, he sat in a special suite to watch a football game alongside then-President-elect Donald Trump and then-Vice President-elect JD Vance.

In 2015, after police apprehended white supremacist Dylann Storm Roof for murdering nine people in a Black church, they made a stop at Burger King to feed him because he was hungry.[32] In December 2024, a militarized squadron of New York Police Department officers, clad in tactical gear and armed with machine guns, escorted Mangione to a Manhattan courthouse in a highly theatrical perp walk as he arrived in the city from Pennsylvania. Then–New York City Mayor Eric Adams was present for the photo op, too. Adams himself had just been indicted months earlier on charges of federal fraud, bribery, and solicitation of a contribution by a foreign national. He spent the entirety of his single term as mayor slashing funding for lifesaving public programs to further bolster an NYPD that largely spends its days chasing (and sometimes shooting) subway fare evaders.[33]

Roof, whose horrifying manifesto detailed his goal of inciting a "race war," didn't face terrorism charges. Mangione's 262-word "manifesto" notably railed against the cruelty and violence of the for-profit health insurance industry.

So, who gets to "have a family"? A similar question, phrased only slightly differently: Whose lives matter and whose are expendable under capitalism and imperialism?

Shortly after Thompson's death, New York Governor Kathy Hochul's administration proposed a hotline devoted to CEOs who felt threatened or unsafe in the aftermath of Thompson's death. The most that school shooting survivors are offered is "thoughts and prayers." Within days of Thompson's death, a Florida mother of two was arrested and jailed for telling her insurance company, "Delay, deny, depose. You people are next," on the phone. She was held on $100,000 bail.[34]

Necropolitics, a framework developed by the Cameroonian historian Achille Mbembe, describes the systems of social and political power that determine who lives and who dies, and how these systems determine which lives are valued and which are regarded—via policy and culture—as disposable. Race and class and geography, proximity to resources, proximity to power, proximity to health and comfort and stability, are key determinants of lifespan. Poor people, people of color, mentally ill and unhoused Black men who are in crisis on public transit—their lives are deemed expendable under American capitalism, colonialism, and white supremacy. Their suffering and death—all easily preventable, with even marginal redistributions of wealth and resources in society—do not go against the grain in any way. Their suffering stems from the system working as designed. A wealthy CEO killed to send a message to the capitalist class, to challenge their feelings of safety while stealing everything from all of us, very much *does* go against the grain of the world in which we live, and must be punished by the state accordingly.

■ ■ ■

Brian Thompson's murder so rattled those in power because, in some ways, it was natural and unsurprising. A shock to the system, certainly—but is a shock to the system, now and then, really so surprising when the system is as rightfully loathed as it is?

You don't have to agree with the UnitedHealthcare shooter's actions. But even if you disagree, it's vital to understand state violence, structural violence, the administrative and bureaucratic violence of an insurance company denying coverage, *as* violent. Revolutionary violence—violence against those at the helm of the very violent systems that are threatening or poisoning your own life—can then be understood as self-defense. The guillotine of the French Revolution, appraised from this angle or that, becomes a symbol of self-defense; it is self-defense against the tyranny and systematic murder and oppression inflicted by monarchy and wealth hoarding. To those who benefit from wealth hoarding, or perhaps those who do not fully conceptualize how much has been stolen from them, how much their lives have been shrunk and worsened by capitalism, the guillotine is terrorism, and Luigi Mangione's terrorism charge is deserved.

The capitalist class sees Mangione and his symbolic power as an existential threat. His actions established a chilling context. When you recognize that a tiny minority of people have taken everything from us and erected a playground for themselves amid an endless abyss of human suffering for which they're entirely responsible, the natural conclusion one reaches is that those who have positioned themselves at the top of this pyramid have to pay; that nothing is going to change until we make them; that no one, unless made to do so by force, would freely give up power; that the consequences of them continuing to hold power are life or death for so many of us.

The capitalist class subsists off a manufactured crisis of cultural illiteracy about state violence. This illiteracy instills in us that there is only one way to kill someone, and that is interpersonally—with a gun, or a knife, or cold hands around the throat. In reality, people, often vulnerable underclasses, are murdered every day by a state that withholds our most basic human needs to enrich the capitalist class, and ensure that capitalists can always profit off not just our labor but our attempts to live. This illiteracy and failure to recognize different forms of violence are akin to object impermanence, the idea that if you cannot see someone or something then it isn't there, that if someone isn't shot in front of you, they weren't murdered. This sanitizes and erases the murders committed by policy and bureaucracy.

Thanks to this illiteracy, powerful institutions that thrive off the existing order—in which profiteers of mass death endlessly enrich themselves by gatekeeping the basic needs we all rely on to survive—can easily misrepresent victims' resistance to oppressive systems as the only aggression taking place. Obsessive demonization of Mangione has, by design, obscured how the for-profit insurance industry is itself the ultimate aggressor.

So: Who gets to have a family? What is violence, and what is self-defense? Does self-defense exist outside of the context of interpersonal abuse? And if it does, what does it look like?

Under the logic of American necropolitics, Luigi Mangione is the terrorist—not Brian Thompson, whose very profession subsisted off profiting from mass death and suffering; not John Fetterman, who routinely votes to fund and arm an apartheid regime that is committing genocide. Because Thompson's life matters, but Jordan Neely's does not; because CEOs, as a class, matter, but Palestinian children, Palestinians writ large, do not.

Indeed, as usual, Palestine is the most shining, crushing example of the rot of Western, imperialist hypocrisies, and the astounding state violence that enforces these hypocrisies. These hypocrisies separate whose families are real and pitiable, and whose families are classified as expected casualties, whose suffering and losses are unimportant by design under capitalism and imperialism, easily if not automatically ignored.

"My love for you is deeper than anything I have ever known. Loving you is not separate from the struggle for liberation," Khalil told his son. "It is liberation itself. I fight for you, and for every Palestinian child whose life deserves safety, tenderness and freedom. I hope one day you will stand tall knowing your father was not absent out of apathy, but out of conviction."

"One day, you might ask why people are punished for standing up for Palestine, why truth and compassion feel dangerous to power," he continued. "These are hard questions, but I hope our story shows you this: the world needs more courage, not less. It needs people who choose justice over convenience."

5

THE RIGHT TO "DUE PROCESS"

Poison a person, go to jail, they call you a felon for life. Poison a city resulting in dozens of deaths and thousands with brain damage, get a teaching fellowship at Harvard, they call you ex-Gov of Michigan Rick Snyder.

—DAVE MCKENNA

In 2022, Tracy McCarter, a Black mother and grandmother who was jailed for killing her estranged, abusive husband in self-defense, had the murder charge against her dismissed after two long years navigating the criminal legal system. She'd spent six months jailed on Rikers Island but was later released on electronic monitoring amid the Covid pandemic, as local activists pressed the district attorney's office to drop the case. "Dismissing the unjust charge against me can't give back what I've lost, but I am relieved that this nightmare is over, and I am determined to once again thrive," McCarter said at the time.[1]

Stories like McCarter's are all too common. Criminalized survivors are incarcerated all across the country for the survival "crime" of killing or harming their abusers in self-defense, or for other circumstances related to the abuse they survived.

Toward the end of his term, President Joe Biden oversaw the largest act of presidential clemency on a single day in modern history. But Biden ultimately neglected to meet a pressing demand among civil and women's rights activists in the final days of his presidency, failing to pardon criminalized survivors.[2] By contrast, Biden *did* issue a full, unconditional pardon to his son Hunter Biden, who had been convicted of illegally buying and possessing a gun while using drugs and also pleaded guilty to nine tax offenses. Biden's justification for pardoning his son made enough sense: His family has long been subject to unwarranted political attacks. But victims of gender-based violence who are imprisoned for trying to survive are also victims of political persecution and were denied the same grace and humanity.

Survivors of Federal Correctional Institution (FCI) Dublin, California, who remain incarcerated, pleaded with the outgoing president to consider granting them clemency. FCI Dublin, a women's prison that staffers dubbed the "rape club" before it closed, gained notoriety for having one of the most pervasive prison sexual abuse scandals in modern history.[3] In 2022, the prison's warden and chaplain were convicted of sexual crimes against incarcerated women following the testimony of whistleblowers, while dozens of employees were placed on leave and remain under investigation. The prison permanently closed in 2024, about two years after reports about widespread misconduct, dispersing its residents to other prisons across the country. Some of the women told *The Guardian* in 2024 that recovering from the trauma they experienced at Dublin is impossible while still incarcerated and expressed fear of retaliation for their roles as whistleblowers.[4]

These women included Roberta Bell, a lead plaintiff in the class-action lawsuit against the US Bureau of Prisons over conditions at Dublin. Bell had previously detailed surviving years of childhood sexual abuse; she was convicted of witness tampering, a firearm charge, and other offenses in a 1992 murder case, but she says her abusive partner coerced her to accompany him to the crime. Bell has been in prison for more than three decades and has never met her grandchildren.

Another Dublin survivor, identified by *The Guardian* as Leslie, alleged that a guard sexually abused her for two years at the Dublin prison; and even after the prison closed, she continued to face the threat of deportation over a drug conviction. One Dublin survivor, Aimee Chavira, who was also convicted on drug charges, received compassionate release in 2023. But despite therapy, she continues to struggle with severe PTSD from FCI Dublin.

Becki Truscott Kondkar, director of Tulane Law School Domestic Violence Clinic and founding co-director of the school's Women's Prison Project, routinely works with criminalized survivors. Kondkar told me in 2024 that clemency, which can come in the form of a commuted sentence or a full pardon, can serve as "an important stopgap when we run out of options" to free survivors within a criminal legal system that seemingly targets them by design. But she stressed that the circumstances at FCI Dublin weren't isolated—prison sexual violence is rampant, and clemency is only a small piece of much bigger solutions that remain necessary. "Incarcerated women are usually invisible to the world, and their stories are rarely told," she added. "In a criminal legal system with so few legal remedies available to incarcerated people after their convictions are final, clemency serves a critical function to redress the system's failures and abuses."

A US Senate report in 2022 showed in at least two-thirds of federal women's prisons, staff have sexually abused incarcerated residents over the previous decade.[5] That same year, New York passed a law expanding the statute of limitations for sex crimes, which gave victims a onetime opportunity to file civil suits. Within days of the law taking effect, one single law firm connected with 750 individuals who said they were sexually assaulted by state prison staff.

In 2012, Marissa Alexander defended herself from her abusive husband by firing a warning shot that caused no physical harm. She was prosecuted and sentenced to a mandatory minimum sentence of twenty years in prison before eventually being freed in 2015 in the face of public outrage. In 2014, Nan-Hui Jo escaped her abusive, American citizen partner and took her young child to seek safety. She was arrested for child abduction and portrayed by prosecutors as a violent "illegal immigrant" attempting to game US systems, rather than a victim; she initially faced indefinite detention, but was later sentenced to 175 days in county jail and released on time served in 2015. Perhaps most famously, Cyntoia Brown was sentenced to fifteen years in prison for killing a man she was forced into sexual relations with when she was sixteen years old. Then–Tennessee Governor Bill Haslam, a Republican, granted Brown clemency in 2019.[6]

"Prisons replicate intimate partner violence on a larger scale. They sometimes replicate the abusive circumstances that may have played a major role in someone's trajectory to prison. Sexual violence is ubiquitous in there," Kondkar said. "Even if there were therapeutic interventions available [to incarcerated survivors], remaining in that setting would make it impossible for that therapy to be useful. There's no possibility of receiving the trauma-informed care needed to recover from abuse in prisons."

These are systemic issues that "can't be addressed with clemency," Kondkar said. Kondkar further told me that clemency is sometimes rendered less applicable to the experiences of criminalized survivors. "It's usually based on acknowledging that someone changed over time and deserves a second chance," she explained. But criminalized survivors are unjustly punished for surviving gender-based violence in the first place. "So, they don't usually show the remorse" that clemency sometimes requires, Kondkar said, "because that would require them to have remorse for surviving."

In 2023, several years after the height of the MeToo movement's prominence in the mainstream, I published my book *Survivor Injustice: State-Sanctioned Abuse, Domestic Violence, and the Fight for Bodily Autonomy*. My book's thesis was simple: Contrary to liberal activism that erroneously framed gender-based violence almost entirely as interpersonal acts by abusive individuals, all too often, gendered abuse manifests as state violence; the state independently functions as an abuser itself, and systematically empowers abusive partners, too. Think: Being unable to leave an abusive partner or family member because you rely on them for health insurance coverage in a capitalist economic system; simultaneously being unable to vote for policy change that might help you escape an abuser, because they won't allow you to vote; being forced to navigate a legal system that retraumatizes victims who come forward against their abusers, and allows abusers to sue and bankrupt victims for "defamation."

You don't have to be an abolitionist to know that the criminal legal system and American policing are not just hostile to but actively dangerous for victims and survivors. Sexual violence is vastly underreported to law enforcement, in no small part because officers of law enforcement are all too often perpetrators of sexual violence themselves. By design, the American legal system writ large is more likely to recognize the victimhood of abusers than the victimhood of those they harm.

On the criminal side of this system, take, for instance, the sexual-assault-to-prison pipeline. Fewer than 1 percent of rapes lead to convictions,[7] but about 90 percent of incarcerated women—a majority of whom are women of color—are survivors. Sisters Inside, an Australian abolitionist group, coined the term "state sexual assault" in 2001 to frame the state itself as a perpetrator of sexual violence through policing and incarceration.

And, on the civil side, accused men are often unsparing in their pursuit of all legal actions they can take to silence or punish victims who come forward, typically through costly, invasive, and devastating defamation suits. Victims are routinely sued for defamation and bankrupted by abusers, while custody battles for their children routinely punish mothers and children who are abuse victims, among a range of other avenues through which victims are retraumatized and further disempowered. One 2017 study found that when mothers alleged domestic violence in custody cases, fathers won custody 73 percent of the time, and when mothers alleged child abuse, fathers won 69 percent of the time.[8] We're told that, in such cases when fathers are accused of abuse, *they* are the victims—of their wives' unhinged, misandrist schemes, coaching their kids to lie and punish their poor, innocent fathers.

Ironically, progressive and left-wing voices that criticize policing and call for the diversion of funds away from police departments or steps toward decarceration are most often accused of disregarding victims' lives. Amid Zohran Mamdani's campaign for mayor of New York City, opponents resurfaced a 2020 podcast interview in which Mamdani, then running for state Assembly, rightly pointed out that we should rethink sending police to respond to domestic violence or mental health crises: "If somebody is jaywalking, if somebody is surviving, going through domestic violence—there are so many different situations that would be far better handled by people trained to deal with those specific situations, as opposed to an individual with a gun," he said.[9]

In response to the resurfaced clips, the right-wing *Free Press*'s Batya Ungar-Sargon claimed, "Zohran Mamdani wants women to have the shit beaten out of them in the best case scenario, be murdered by their husbands in the worst, in the name of Defund the Police." With zero sense of irony, political commentator Megyn Kelly shared the audio and invoked the case of O. J. and Nicole Simpson—who repeatedly called the police but was still killed while her killer went free. A former NYPD homicide detective called Mamdani's position "absolutely insane," baselessly claiming that "homicide rates will increase, women will be pulverized."

Here, abuse victims' very identities are weaponized to uphold an innately abusive system that actively threatens their lives. It's hard to think of any class of people that poses a greater danger to abuse victims than the police. About one quarter of victims who call 911 over a domestic violence incident are arrested or threatened with arrest themselves. The National Domestic Violence Hotline's 2022 report found 70 percent of victim survey respondents who called police say they regret their decision and wouldn't contact the police again.[10] Victims, as a class, are far more likely to be jailed than their rapists and abusers: It's estimated that just 3 percent of rapists will ever spend a day in jail, whereas, again, about 90 percent of incarcerated women are survivors.[11]

The available data indicating just how detrimental policing is to victims' safety is overwhelming. Between 65 and 85 percent of sexual assaults are unreported,[12] often because victims fear police—they fear that they themselves will be punished, or they fear the prospect of sending someone else to prison. Even if rape victims do report their experiences, and even if they are believed, many are ultimately retraumatized for nothing: Hundreds of thousands of rape kits sit untested across the country. Police and prison staff are frequently perpetrators of gender-based violence themselves, placing any victims who turn to them for help at risk. At least 40 percent of police officers have self-reported as domestic abusers. Most prison rapes are committed by guards and staff. Sexual abuse is the second-most common act of police misconduct.

And, to be clear, the minuscule percentage of reported rapes that are labeled false is likely a significant overcount: A 1996 report compiling police data indicating 8 percent of rapes are falsely reported is a result of the FBI marking rapes and sexual assaults that didn't involve a weapon, or were reported by people who had a prior relationship with their assailants (which is most assaults), as "false reports," Amia Srinivasan found in researching her 2021 book, *The Right to Sex*.[13] And when false accusations and reports happen, they overwhelmingly involve district attorneys or police officers pressuring victims to identify a certain man as their rapist or attacker, in order to close cases and inflate their safety records. So, supposed "false reports" may happen, but they aren't coming from the stereotypical, vengeful, lying woman invented by our rabidly anti-feminist cultural imagination—but from the state itself.

It should not be a radical position to state that police aren't trained or equipped to respond to domestic violence situations, and sending them is exactly what leads to tragedies like that of Gabby Petito, whom police treated as the abuser while treating her eventual killer as her victim.[14] Speaking of Petito's case, which saw officers high-five her future killer and put him up in a hotel while making Petito spend the night in her van just days before her death: One of the officers involved in this confrontation had allegedly threatened to kill his ex-girlfriend while working as a cop in a different city—and he was still working as a cop when he encountered Petito in 2021.[15]

In the summer of 2020, amid a nationwide uprising for racial justice, nearly fifty anti–sexual violence organizations signed the "Moment of Truth" letter highlighting the harms of police and prisons on victims of abuse and calling for divestment from the carceral system. Soon after sharing the letter, some of the groups who co-signed it, including local shelters and community anti-violence programs, lost public funding, while others said police departments stopped referring victims to their services.[16]

There is also no shortage of examples of police officers exploiting their state power to stalk, harass, sexually violate, and even kill women—and these are just the cases we know of. Over the last decade, cops in Arizona, Georgia, Kansas, Maryland, and other states have been exposed for stalking local women. In 2020, the parents of Lauren McCluskey, a Utah woman who was denied a restraining order against her ex-boyfriend and later killed by him, filed a lawsuit against police officers, alleging they'd shared nude photos of McCluskey. In Oklahoma, an officer named Daniel

Holtzclaw was imprisoned for stalking and sexually assaulting more than a dozen Black women from 2013 to 2014.[17]

Relatedly, race and class play an indelible role in how police and the legal system writ large treat victims. Take, for example, the political and cultural impact of laws like the Violence Against Women Act, and the exclusionary, racialized activism that led to its passage in the 1990s. Prior to VAWA, domestic violence was widely accepted, normalized, and shrugged off as a private matter, exclusively discussed in underground, feminist consciousness-raising circles. Advocacy on behalf of gender-based violence victims began to draw mainstream support amid the tough-on-crime era in the 1980s and 1990s, when awareness campaigns on the issue conflated it with "stranger danger" violence in the streets.[18] Of course, most gender-based violence is carried out by intimate partners or someone the victim knows, and often takes place at home or otherwise in private. As public awareness and protest of gender-based violence increased, some of the movement's most visible activists abandoned its more radical demands to gain wider public support, resulting in collusion with law enforcement and the carceral features of laws like VAWA.

Eventually, VAWA was introduced as part of then-Senator Joe Biden's 1994 crime bill. Among a range of problems with the law—which, in some ways, put victims at greater risk—VAWA allocates most of its funding to police departments to respond to domestic violence, despite their long histories of disbelieving, mistreating, and retraumatizing survivors. VAWA requires that an arrest be made when someone calls the police to report experiencing domestic violence, and can result in victims themselves being criminalized and arrested, sometimes if police officers deem them the primary aggressor, and other times to compel them to testify against their abuser if they're afraid to cooperate with law enforcement.

We have seen that courtrooms are hardly a friendlier environment for victims and survivors than police stations are. Survivors are routinely disbelieved and punished for their own testimonies about the gender-based violence to which they've been subjected. As I note earlier in this book, in 2022, the civil trial held to determine whether actress Amber Heard defamed her ex-husband, Johnny Depp, by writing an op-ed about surviving domestic violence, offered a chilling glimpse into the legal system's (and general public's) cruelty. Heard, herself, was portrayed by Depp's legal team as abusive for reacting to and fighting back against his abuse. Their trial presented a textbook case of DARVO.

On college campuses, defamation suits have long targeted student survivors who report their assaults. In 2021, Know Your IX published a report based on more than 100 interviews with campus sexual assault survivors who had been victimized between 2002 and 2020, and found almost a quarter of them were threatened with a defamation suit from their attacker. Nearly one in five said they were warned by their school of the possibility of defamation suits, and 10 percent faced "retaliatory complaints" filed by their assailants.[19] A Know Your IX organizer and co-author of the 2021 report told me about a student whose assailant was expelled from her university—only for him to file a defamation lawsuit that allowed him to "access her medical records, school records, even her sexual history," forcing her to transfer schools, delay her graduation, and spend more than $100,000 out of pocket. In 2022, for *Jezebel*, I reported on a rising tide of increasingly successful "anti-male bias" lawsuits in response to disciplinary action around campus sexual assaults. One database claimed at the time that more than 700 Title IX–related lawsuits had been filed since 2013, though it wasn't clear how many had been thrown out or privately settled.[20]

In 2017, at the onset of the MeToo movement, Pamela Lopez, a California-based lobbyist, joined numerous women working in state politics to speak out against the prevalence of sexual harassment in their line of work. She testified before the legislature that she'd been assaulted by a state lawmaker the year before, and while speaking, she was pressed to reveal his name—a demand that would spark an avalanche of legal action against her. Lopez named her assailant, then-Assemblymember Matt Dababneh, which was protected speech. But Dababneh then sued her for naming him at a press conference after her testimony. A court initially ruled that her remarks during the press conference were not protected speech in 2018, but a federal appeals court ruled in her favor in 2021. Yet, by that point, the damage was largely done. Lopez told me:

> Every Christmas, every holiday, every birthday, almost four years, I had the weight of this terrible lawsuit hanging over my head. This guy [Dababneh] was absolutely out for blood, to destroy my reputation, spreading rumors about me, slut-shaming me.[23]

Over the course of the legal harassment campaign Dababneh inflicted on Lopez, she told me she learned that several other women had accused him of sexual assault. Still, he saw himself as "the real victim" at her hands, specifically, because her testimony had inspired others to speak up too. "He could have just not assaulted anyone," she said. "But I'm the one who was punished, I'm the one who was wrong, for trying to get justice."

Jessica Stender, policy director at the gender justice nonprofit Equal Rights Advocates, told me in 2023 that about one year after Heard and Depp's defamation trial, her organization was "seeing a huge increase in these types of legal attacks, of predators trying to weaponize the law and the courts against survivors when they speak out." And, "even if, ultimately, the survivor would win in this type of retaliatory defamation suit" like Lopez, Stender told me, this best-case scenario arises "only after years of really time-consuming, expensive, and deeply retraumatizing litigation that survivors should never have been put through in the first place."

In 2023, California passed A.B. 933, a law that makes it substantially more difficult for abusers to sue and exploit the legal system to harass their victims. The law amended California's civil code to treat "communications made without malice regarding sexual assault, harassment, or discrimination" as privileged speech.[22] This doesn't sweepingly stop these lawsuits from happening, particularly if a judge determines someone's public allegations of abuse *are* made with malice. But if the victim wins the defamation suit against them, under A.B. 933, the person suing them will be liable to pay their legal fees. The law marks a crucial step in the right direction to protect victims from costly, highly destabilizing legal harassment. But the very need for a law like this, at all, speaks volumes about the targeted, gendered violence that is innate to our legal system, how tools that abusers can wield to punish their victims are innate to this system and all too often go unrectified.

The National Sexual Violence Resource Center estimates the lifetime economic cost of rape across all US victims stands at nearly $3.1 trillion, including $1.2 trillion in medical costs and $234 billion in legal costs.[23] On their own, the medical bills associated with experiencing gender-based violence are alarming: A 2022 study analyzed national data from almost thirty-six million emergency-room visits in 2019 and found costs for sexual assault–related visits averaged $3,551 for all victims, while pregnant victims faced an even higher average charge: $4,553.19.[24]

Defamation suits are still just one dimension of terror that abusers can inflict on their victims through the legal system. While writing *Survivor Injustice*, I interviewed several women who had children they conceived from rape and were then subjected to years of agonizing—and costly—abuse in custody courts. Sharing a child with your abuser can link you to them for the rest of your life. And that's exactly why impregnating their victims, with or without their consent, is such a common line of attack from abusers. In some states, including several that have banned abortion, a divorce can't be finalized while someone is pregnant, without exceptions for abuse. In February 2024, researchers published a paper in which they estimated that in fourteen states that had banned abortion after

Dobbs v. Jackson Women's Health, there had been 64,565 rape-induced pregnancies—primarily in states whose abortion bans lacked rape exceptions.[25] Unless their rapist has been criminally convicted, many of these women struggle to gain full custody; even if they invoke the abuse they suffered in family court, or their children testify about being abused, as I noted earlier in this chapter, the father may be *more* likely to win custody. The father is the victim, because he is being denied fatherhood—all while wielding the courts to further torture his victim.

In 2023, *The New Yorker*'s Eren Orbey interviewed Lucy Guarnera, a psychology researcher at the University of Virginia who frequently interviews women who have endured custody battles with their rapists. Guarnera told him:

> I had multiple participants talk about rapist fathers who, while they were pregnant, or shortly after they gave birth, threatened them or blackmailed them and said, "Hey, if you go to police, or you continue cooperating with police, I am going to make your life a living hell. I am going to get custody and visitation access to your child, I'm never going to stop until I have full custody. You better drop that criminal case right now." In some circumstances, this worked.

She continued, "I don't know if a 'power trip' is the word I'm looking for, but I think that's what it is and it's all just for power. Isn't that what sexual assault is? You just want to overpower your victim."[26]

■ ■ ■

In 2023, I learned the term "himpathy" from reading Dr. Nicole Bedera's research. She presented the term in a paper, and about a year later, developed that paper into a book entitled *On the Wrong Side: How Universities Protect Perpetrators and Betray Survivors of*

Sexual Violence. "Himpathy" describes excessive sympathy for men at the expense of women. Case in point: A male student might be expelled for punching another male student; but if a male student is accused of violence by a female student, that male student is by default regarded as the victim of a gendered witch hunt.

College campuses are often sites of harsh administrative cruelty toward survivors, weaponizing the worst and most prejudiced aspects of the American legal system. Through observation at one large public university's Title IX office between 2018 and 2019, and seventy-six interviews with Title IX administrators and students at the unnamed university, Bedera found that in most cases, Title IX administrators determined the trauma that victims incurred was either too severe for the university to even try to remedy, or that the women were "hysterical." Sometimes administrators determined that neither party was lying when they had different perspectives on how a sexual encounter had transpired. But in such cases, men's proclamations of innocence were valued above women saying they were violated. An attitude that assailants are unfairly punished for engaging in typical "boys will be boys" behavior also prevailed. "There's this myth that men's lives are ruined when they're accused of sexual violence—it isn't just untrue, it becomes the justification for giving them benefits, for giving them more power and privilege as the result of the sexual violence they commit, to compensate for that notion," Bedera told me.

Her book features well over a dozen deeply unsettling anecdotes through interviews with the victims, the accused students, and the administrators overseeing these cases. I'd like to highlight one case in particular.

Bedera met and interviewed "Justin" and "Marissa" (all names throughout her book are pseudonyms) a year after their case closed. Both were participants in Greek life, and even though Marissa reported Justin for rape and Justin denied the allegation, their narratives about what happened are similar. They both agree that Marissa stated early on that she did not want to have sexual intercourse. They both agree that Justin penetrated her later in the night despite this. They both agree that Justin also became violent with her, hitting her with his belt and choking her. They only disagree on whether a violation took place.

Justin's "proof" of consent is that he and Marissa discussed her birth control method and their last STI tests, and that Marissa removed her clothing and consensually engaged in some sex acts with him; he also pointed to her decision to stay the night and her response to his texts the next day saying she enjoyed their night together. Marissa recounted repeatedly asking Justin to stop, performing the sex acts he wanted because she feared for her life as he became more violent, and continuing to respond to his advances over text as she remained fearful for her safety. This, Bedera wrote, is a common and well-documented trauma response among victims—but none of the Title IX administrators had backgrounds in sexual violence research and none understood this.

The Title IX office sided with Justin seemingly from the get-go. As is the standard at the university Bedera observed, once the investigation was underway, Justin was assigned to work with the Dean of Students' office, while Marissa, like all reporting students, worked with the victim advocacy office, which has a total of three employees, a one-room office, and a shoestring budget. The school agreed to Marissa's request for a no-contact order to protect her from Justin's harassment. But the supposedly equal application of the order meant Marissa couldn't talk about her case on threat of expulsion, so she couldn't reach out to witnesses or warn other women about Justin's predatory behavior—even as she quickly learned from classmates in her dance program that Justin had harmed or even assaulted them, too. Meanwhile, the Dean of Students' office maintained that Justin had a right to defend his reputation, allowing him to turn most Greek life students against Marissa and smear her as, in her words, "psycho" and "a ho."

As he worked closely with the Dean of Students' office, which is well funded and staffed with some of the most powerful figures at the university, Justin built close relationships with them, and they accommodated nearly all of his requests. He was able to retroactively drop classes he'd failed, from semesters prior to the Title IX investigation. He was able to smear Marissa as a means of "self-defense," all while she was threatened with expulsion for warning other women about his violent behaviors. (Bedera found that at least one student accused of rape was granted funding from the Dean of Students' office to fly halfway across the country to go to his family home.)

For Marissa, the Title IX investigation process required a significant amount of labor, mental energy, exhaustive scheduling inconveniences, and more, all on top of the trauma and social ostracism she had to navigate. But any requests for accommodations from her were perceived by Title IX administrators as evidence that she was lying and had simply reported Justin to advantage herself. Administrators eventually, predictably favored Justin; Justin told Bedera he enjoyed "humiliating" Marissa by making her read her texts about enjoying their night together aloud in front of administrators at one point in the process. Marissa appealed but ultimately dropped the case, when the exhaustive toll it took made her realize her choices were to either continue pursuing it or graduate. The organization Know Your IX reports that 39 percent of survivors who report are forced to take a leave of absence, transfer, or drop out due to the toll of the reporting process on their education.

Justin and Marissa's case reflects key themes from Bedera's research. It's also the only case Bedera studied in which a victim appealed, because most students quickly learn from the initial investigation that the process is stacked against them. And this case ultimately embodies how the Title IX process routinely tortures, humiliates, and retraumatizes victims; it forces them to feel guilty, or as if they're faking their victimhood for supposed benefits, when they merely ask for help while enduring the process. Meanwhile, not only are perpetrators rarely ever sanctioned, but university administrators often feel so guilty for putting them through the investigative process that they grant accused students any accommodations they ask for, all while denying victims' requests. There couldn't be a more overt example of how DARVO is institutionalized and normalized, how victims are cast as abusers, and abusers as victims—how victims are further harmed while abusers are further empowered, under the guise of rendering justice.

"The most common outcome is an insufficient evidence finding, and in those cases, the school really does perceive the perpetrator as someone who was falsely accused, whose time was wasted, and that they owe the perpetrator something," Bedera explained. "And that's where a lot of these benefits come from."

At the university that Bedera studied, she found the school suspends 3.29 students per year for gender-based violence; they expel just 0.71 students. The Title IX office received close to 500 reports during Bedera's year at the university. Of those reports, a student was suspended or expelled just 1 percent of the time; the only perpetrator who was expelled that year, Bedera wrote, was expelled for threatening physical harm against a Title IX administrator.

"After the MeToo movement, something that people are really having a hard time wrapping their heads around is this sense of, once we know that a man is violent, aren't we doing something about it? But we've seen the opposite: They get more and more power, especially on campus, where they now have the arm of the institution assisting and enabling their abuse," Bedera said. "And once men have that kind of power, these kinds of benefits, it only becomes easier to perpetrate violence."

Bedera argues that "himpathy" is universal across how institutions appear to respond to reports of sexual violence from women against men. "There was this real sense within all of the offices that the employees needed to do their work neutrally. But . . . because there is a huge power disparity between victim and perpetrator," she explained, "if you treat victim and perpetrator the same, you will always be enabling the perpetrator and empowering them to have more power over the victim."

Bedera also wrote about June, a graduate theater student whose partner raped and abused her over the course of months. He was also a theater student, who had a close relationship with their male professor, as this professor treasured the rarity of straight, male theater students. June's abuser, too, was serially accused of a wide range of violent and predatory behaviors toward their classmates. But the Title IX office suggested June had somehow coordinated this barrage of allegations, rather than coming to the more likely conclusion that her abuser was a serial predator, and also determined that since the abusive acts were wide-ranging, they couldn't point to a pattern of predatory behavior.

One administrator told Bedera that reported Title IX cases typically involved mere disagreements and misunderstandings about whether there was consent: "If you feel icky about it, you can feel icky about it. . . . But that also doesn't mean you have to be mad at someone else," they said. One administrator told Bedera she believed a victim was only reporting her assailant as "revenge" for his infidelity, ignoring a death threat the assailant had sent the victim.

In reality, survivors wanted housing accommodations so they no longer had to live with or near their abuser, they wanted protective orders so they wouldn't have to see their rapist every day in class or at campus organization meetings. They wanted to feel safe. Instead, universities and institutions treat their reports as innate threats to men, and opt to shield these accused men accordingly.

Notably, one administrator told Bedera that he "always had this perception that [sexual assault] only happens with a creeper in the bushes that jumps out," and that many of the cases he's worked on involve "bad behavior" but were "perhaps not predatory." This "stranger danger" framing of sex crimes emerged in the 1970s "tough on crime" era, mischaracterizing sexual assailants exclusively as men of color and strangers to justify further investments in policing. Instead, most acts of sexual violence are committed by people the victims know. But Title IX administrators couldn't conceptualize predominantly white, privileged, male college students as violent criminals, because they didn't fit the racialized, stereotyped imagery of the "creeper in the bushes."

Bedera's research exposes not just a broader culture of corruption and impunity in the institution of academia—it also exposes, more broadly, who is and isn't allowed to rape in the white supremacist, elitist imagination. The "creeper in the bushes," coded as Black or brown and emerging from the "streets," is reviled as a criminal and rapist, whereas the middle- or upper-class college student, coded as white and wealthy, is simply misunderstood. On top of this, the misunderstood, male college rapist is coded as the victim of *his* victim's conspiracy.

In this sense, the university functions as a microcosm; the anatomy of a campus sexual assault investigation highlights who is and isn't permitted to get away with sexual violence in society and in empire, often along lines of race and privilege. Consider, again, the extensive and well-documented acts of sexual violence perpetrated by Israelis against the Palestinians they have colonized—all while the prevailing narrative centers unsubstantiated stories about a "mass rape campaign" perpetrated by Hamas against Israelis. The "creeper in the bushes" and the misunderstood student are stand-ins for different people's relationships to power and privilege, determining whether they are appraised as victim or abuser.

■ ■ ■

In 2025, the New York Police Department framed itself as the victim of Zohran Mamdani's political ascent.[27] His historic primary victory sparked a wave of "reports" about police planning to leave the city in droves when he took office, because, apparently, New

York would no longer be safe for Candy Crush addicts. (We heard the same about billionaires and CEOs.)

The right-wing panic about what a Mamdani victory could mean for the NYPD stemmed from his history of calls to defund the police. On the campaign trail, Mamdani argued that well-resourced cities, where communities' needs are met because city budgets invest more in services than cops and jails, are safe cities. After all, in recent years, homicide rates have actually dropped across the country[28]—all while people die or suffer tremendously every day because they can't afford health care or housing.

Nonetheless, these right-wing panics are predicated on the delusional conspiracy theory that cops make us safer, a mythology akin to believing in the Tooth Fairy. Calls to move away from policing and incarceration, we're told, are existential threats to "Blue Lives," a protected, marginalized class—and threats to "Blue Lives" are threats to *all* our lives, certainly threats to abuse victims.

But police don't prevent "crime" or violence—they merely (sometimes) respond to it, often inadequately, and often in ways that only worsen or reproduce violence, and all while swallowing up cities' entire budgets, defunding lifesaving resources and civil servants capable of responding to crises without brutalizing anyone. Modern policing in the United States originates from slave patrols, and policing continues that tradition today: Police, by design, do not protect people; they protect capital and private property. They would bulldoze crowds and kill or brutalize human beings in the name of protecting property—they do this quite frequently. Over the course of 2020, as people around the world took to the streets to protest police brutality and assert that Black Lives Matter, in numerous cases across the country, police cars would drive or threaten to drive into crowds. Many were arrested for theft or property damage at the same time that cops faced no accountability for inflicting physical harm on human beings. And, I can't stress this enough: When right-wingers describe the apocalyptic conditions that would arise if cities allocated even a little less funding for police departments, what they're willfully ignoring is that the hellscape crime anecdotes they're citing are happening *right now*, under a status quo of massive funding for police and jails.

Defunding police is, we're told by the right, the most radical position one could possibly take. "Defund the police" is their boogeyman, the slogan blamed for everything that's already happening, right now, with police more funded than any other institution in cities across the United States.

Time and again, activists and movements toward decarceration, or politicians like Mamdani who propose even modest changes to the current system responsible for such massive suffering, are framed as radical. They are put on the defensive, pressured to scale back this proposal or that to seem more "reasonable." But in reality, fascists will smear anything even a hair short of fascism as "radical."

Carceral logic is enabled by a broad, public failure to conceive of violence on a structural level. Grown adults who are still unable to grasp the innate violence of police funding, wealth hoarding, prisons, and the for-profit health care system, for instance, are similar to toddlers who lack object permanence. If you don't slap or murder someone right before their eyes, they don't see the violence. The notion that police, who shoot and kill around a thousand people per year in the United States,[29] should be called on to keep anyone safe is delusional. Just as politicians and CEOs routinely kill or enact structural violence through austerity policies, exploitation, and unfathomable wealth hoarding, police routinely kill and brutalize civilians. But this violence—*state* violence, perpetrated by state actors—isn't seen as criminal or violent at all, because of cops' social and political positioning as agents of the state. Consequently, police remain heralded as the solution to crime and violence when they are in fact the ultimate purveyors of it.

As journalist Dave McKenna wrote in 2020, referencing the ongoing crisis of poisoned water in Flint, Michigan, which itself presents an outrageous example of state violence: "Poison a person, go to jail, they call you a felon for life. Poison a city resulting in dozens of deaths and thousands with brain damage, get a teaching fellowship at Harvard, they call you ex-Gov of Michigan Rick Snyder."[30]

State violence is invisibilized. The current paradigm of police, prisons, and courts relies on public faith in these institutions as our great protectors, the guardian angels of abuse victims and survivors, in particular. Threats to the police state are coded as threats to victims; so, the police state persists, and continues to terrorize victims.

6

THE RIGHT TO VICTIMHOOD

Our country has been ravaged by a horde of illegal aliens molesting American children, battering and bruising and beating up American women, and violently raping American women and girls.

—REP. NANCY MACE

In the summer of 2023, an all-male panel of anti-abortion-movement leaders gathered in Georgia for a weekend of harassing the local abortion clinic and brainstorming strategies to make abortion "unthinkable"—including through advocating for laws that punish abortion patients with the death penalty. These men are abortion "abolitionists," who go against the grain of the mainstream "pro-life" movement and argue that not only should abortion providers face state punishment, but abortion patients should, too. It's an overtly extreme position that most Republican politicians will publicly condemn.[1] But whether or not they openly support the punishment of women and abortion patients, that's what banning abortion and imposing forced pregnancy are: punishment.

At the 2023 panel, End Abortion Now leader Zachary Conover told attendees, "It's a dirty little secret of the pro-life industry . . . the lie that women should be allowed to kill their own children with immunity and impunity because they themselves are victims of abortion. It is a lie that says that they are never legally culpable, however willfully or intentionally they carry out the act of taking the life."

Panelists joined Conover in calling for "equal protection" laws for embryos and fetuses, which would consequently classify them as murder victims, should someone terminate their pregnancy. Abortion "abolitionists," as their name suggests, effectively co-opt the unthinkable oppression of slavery, and in fact frequently invoke both slavery and the Holocaust to compare these institutions to abortion. They frame their movement as liberatory, and the very women they victimize as slaveowners and Nazis. This is a reversal of victim and offender of stunning proportions.

This is how the anti-abortion movement justifies the state torture and, in this case, advocates for the state killing of pregnant women: by positioning these women as the abusers, and their unborn embryos and fetuses as the victims. Abortion bans are, indeed, state torture framed as the defense of fetuses; by the fall of 2024, there were five known cases of women in Georgia and Texas who died from being unable to receive time-sensitive emergency abortions for their fatal pregnancy complications.[2]

By the spring of 2025, about a dozen states introduced legislation in a single session that would classify abortion as homicide—in a handful of these states, homicide is eligible for the death penalty. In 2024, the Texas Republican Party adopted a platform that called for abortion to be recognized as homicide under the state criminal code, effectively advocating for the death penalty for abortion patients. In 2023, five different states (Arkansas, Kentucky, Oklahoma, South Carolina, and Texas) introduced bills in one single month to charge abortion patients with homicide.[3]

Since the *Dobbs v. Jackson Women's Health* ruling that overturned *Roe v. Wade* and ended the federal right to abortion, more than a dozen states have enforced total or near-total abortion bans, even as some of these laws are in and out of court, sometimes enforced, sometimes blocked. Even before *Dobbs*, people were long criminalized for their pregnancy outcomes. From 2006 to 2020, more than 1,300 people faced criminal charges for conduct associated with pregnancy, pregnancy loss, abortion, or birth.[4] But abortion bans, which automatically shroud all pregnancies in potential criminal suspicion, have created ever-greater risk. In the first two years, Pregnancy Justice has tracked more than 400 cases. *Dobbs* and abortion bans have only escalated the innate criminal suspicion attached to pregnancy loss. In the first year after *Dobbs* alone, the organization recorded more than 250 people who were arrested over pregnancy-related criminal charges—the most in a single-year period since the organization had been keeping track. Pregnancy Justice recorded more than 400 arrests within the first two years post-*Dobbs*.[5] Overwhelmingly, pregnancy-related criminal charges don't explicitly involve abortion, but the legal humanization of fetuses, warranting state punishment for the woman's alleged mistreatment of that fetus, which is classified as the victim while she is positioned as the perpetrator.[6]

Dana Sussman, senior vice president of Pregnancy Justice, told me in 2023 that around 97 percent of criminal charges for pregnancy outcomes she's tracked have been for "murder, manslaughter, feticide, child endangerment, abuse of a corpse," even as none of these charges are even meant to criminalize pregnancy outcomes.

When an embryo is considered a "baby," this "[normalizes] the idea that a pregnant person is not their own person anymore, that they're subservient to the rights, individuality, and full personhood of a fetus," Sussman said. All too often, this leads to catastrophic, criminal outcomes for pregnant people: "If their rights are secondary to the fetus, or at odds with the fetus, that lends to an environment in which violence—whether it's state violence like imprisonment, or interpersonal violence—can be committed against pregnant people with far less accountability."

On an interpersonal level, abusive partners can wield the supposed personhood of fetuses to abuse pregnant victims: They can sue for wrongful death over their partners' abortions, for instance.

Since 2023, a handful of men in Texas have taken such legal actions. Or they can prohibit pregnant victims from traveling out of state by accusing them of "kidnapping" the fetus. In a survey published in 2024, the National Domestic Violence Hotline found that out of 3,400 respondents, hundreds of domestic violence victims said their abusive partners threatened to report them to law enforcement or sue them if they had abortions.[7] No abortion bans currently threaten the patient themselves with criminal charges—but because these *are* criminal abortion bans, naturally, many victims assume they can be punished by the state for their abortions. Abusers weaponize these gaps in knowledge, wielding these laws and public confusion about their enforcement mechanisms as another tool in their toolbox.

The humanization of fetuses and their political positioning as "victims" have also served as grounds for unthinkable violence against abortion providers and advocates. In the 1990s alone, seven abortion providers were murdered by anti-abortion extremists. An anti-abortion activist shot and killed Dr. David Gunn in 1993; Dr. John Britton and James Barrett were killed by anti-abortion activists in 1994. As recently as 2009, Dr. George Tiller was murdered by an anti-abortion activist while in church. The numerous high-profile assassinations of abortion providers in the 1990s yielded the FACE Act (Freedom of Access to Clinic Entrances), which prohibits anti-abortion protesters from blocking entry to abortion clinics. Within days of taking office in 2025, Donald Trump effectively greenlit the return of peak levels of anti-abortion violence by pardoning about two dozen anti-abortion protesters who were convicted for not just illegally barricading abortion clinics, but in some cases, violently attacking patients and clinic staff. Center for Reproductive Rights President Nancy Northup called the pardons a "get-out-of-jail-free card inviting anti-abortion extremists to step up their attacks on reproductive health clinics with impunity."[8]

Among the pardoned were anti-abortion leader Lauren Handy and her co-defendants, who, in May 2024, were sentenced to five years in prison for invading a Washington, DC, clinic in 2020. While invading the clinic, one of Handy's co-defendants assaulted a nurse who then sprained her knee; another knocked a woman experiencing labor pains to the floor and then blocked her from entering the clinic. Despite these actions, Trump declared in 2025 that Handy and her co-defendants "should not have been prosecuted" and praised them for being "peaceful pro-life protesters." At the same time, Trump also pardoned hundreds of January 6 insurrectionists, framing them as the victims of a corrupt legal system.[9] Many of these insurrectionists were known in their communities for harassing abortion clinics, and immediately after being pardoned, went on to commit a range of serious crimes, including child sexual abuse.[10]

A spokesperson of the National Abortion Federation (NAF) indeed confirmed to me in 2021 that "some of the people at the January 6 insurrection are the same people who have been targeting abortion providers and protesting at clinics in their communities." And "the people who threaten clinic workers and harass individuals seeking abortion care are often the same people who participate in other violent and extremist activities that are rooted in racism, white supremacy, and misogyny, and are deeply harmful."

In 2023, NAF reported that, in the year *Roe* was overturned, providers saw a 538 percent increase in people obstructing clinic entrances (from forty-five in 2021 to 287 in 2022); a 913 percent increase in stalking of clinic staff (from eight in 2021 to eighty-one in 2022); and a 144 percent increase in bomb threats. In 2021, per NAF's tracking, providers reported a 125 percent increase (between 2019 and 2020) in assaults and altercations instigated by anti-abortion protesters, including "shoving, pushing, tripping, and spitting on clinic escorts, staff, and others outside of clinics." Between 1977 and 2024, there were eleven murders and twenty-six attempted murders of providers by anti-abortion extremists, according to NAF.[11]

Anti-abortion politicians often attempt to distance themselves from more overt anti-abortion violence against providers and patients, as we saw in the immediate aftermath of the 2015 mass shooting at a Planned Parenthood clinic in Colorado by a man who later said he "killed three and saved 3,000 babies."[12] But however "pro-life" politicians may claim to be, when they equate a health service and ending an unwanted pregnancy to killing a baby, they're inviting violence against people who offer and have abortions—and they know it.

This is the shared logic of so-called abortion "abolitionists" and the anti-abortion movement writ large: that abortion is murder. The very existence of their movement functionally places targets on women's and abortion providers' backs—all of this predicated on playing the victim, on humanizing and attaching victimhood to embryos.

Sometimes, anti-abortion leaders do label abortion seekers and patients as "victims"—but only to then enact further harm upon them. Long before *Dobbs*, states passed restriction after restriction on abortion, all justified by faux concerns for "women's safety." Many of these laws imposed medically unnecessary requirements on abortion clinics that consequently shut them down. Research has revealed a direct link between anti-abortion laws that shut down clinics and a higher rate of domestic violence–related homicide, as well as between anti-abortion laws and higher maternal mortality and morbidity rates.

Still, these laws—and, today, total abortion bans—were passed in the name of "protecting women" and potential, so-called "victims" of the "abortion industry."

Some of the most successful far-right political movements in the United States have relied on abusive self-victimization narratives from oppressive institutions to justify the scaling back of varying underclasses' basic human rights, framing these underclasses as the aggressors.

The anti-abortion movement is certainly one of these far-right movements.

■ ■ ■

We encounter these same tactics—reversing victim and offender to justify state violence, framing those who hold the least societal power as towering monsters and predators endangering women and children—in the fascist war on queer and trans people. Right-wing propaganda portrays trans women as abusers to cis women and girls not through any actions, but through their very existence. Ironically, some of the most vocal and politically powerful transphobes (like President Trump) are sexual assailants themselves, yet, all the time, conservative parents are all too happy to parade their children alongside Trump, in the vicinity of an alleged child sexual predator, for photo ops.

In 2024 alone, the Trans Legislation Tracker counted almost 700 anti-trans bills in state legislatures across the country—more than any previous year on record.[13] Those bills included invasive attacks on trans people's access to bathrooms as well as attacks on gender-affirming care, particularly for minors. In Congress, Republicans introduced eighty anti-trans bills in 2024, according to tracking by The 19th news.[14] The last decade since the Supreme Court legalized same-sex marriage in 2015 has been defined by a steady, sharpening rise in retaliatory, anti-LGBTQ legislation—most of which is predicated on bigoted caricatures of LGBTQ adults as innate sexual predators, of health providers who offer gender-affirming care to young people as sexual assailants, of trans women who use the restrooms that correspond with their gender as potential rapists.

This propaganda has fueled a range of state and federal legislation, from bans on trans youth participation in sports, to bans on youth gender-affirming care, to the removal of trans women from women's prisons, rerouting them to men's prisons, where they face certain sexual violence, brutality, and possibly death, all sanctioned by the state. All of the aforementioned policies, in fact, are state-sanctioned violence—how else are bans on trans youth participation in sports enforced but through either the mandated inspection of children's genitals or the implicit threat of such inspections?

Yet, without any basis, Trump and other anti-trans politicians aggressively push the claim that trans girls participating in sports threaten the safety and even lives of cis girls. Playing sports, in general, comes with safety risks—that's the nature of competitive physical activity. And no one poses a greater danger to cis or trans girls than politically powerful sexual predators who are obsessed with children's genitals.

In one of Donald Trump's first moves as president in his second term, he signed an executive order attempting to erase trans people. The order claimed to "restore biological truth" and, consequently, mandated that incarcerated trans women be relocated to men's facilities and be denied access to gender transition treatments. Immediately, three incarcerated trans women were removed from the general population of their women's prison and placed in segregated housing. Despite their and their families' pleas, they were told by the Federal Bureau of Prisons that they would soon be moved to men's prisons. The women filed a lawsuit to stop their removal, pointing out that if they're moved to a men's facility, they'll face high risk of sexual violence and death.

Prisons are already rife with sexual violence, often perpetrated by prison staff, and trans incarcerated people are at substantially higher risk of sexual violence. Family members of one of the plaintiffs wrote to the bureau that transferring her to a men's prison would be "the end of her," adding, "She will get sexually assaulted and even possibly killed for being who she is. She is a citizen designated as a female and deserves protection like any other human. . . . This could mean life or death and she has not received a death penalty as her sentence." Throughout Trump's presidency, as lawsuits like this are shuffled around the court system, incarcerated trans women's lives will hang in limbo.

Trans people ask only for the right to exist as themselves. In response, they are characterized as monsters and subjected to unthinkable violence. Popular conservative influencers like the viral Libs of TikTok account have galvanized bomb threats and mass harassment campaigns against children's hospitals that provide youth gender-affirming care, and local schools and libraries that offer inclusive spaces for LGBTQ people, as well as hate campaigns against queer and trans teachers. Often enough, the cruelty is the point: Under the Trump presidency, any acknowledgment of queer and trans existence was scrubbed from federal web pages, and the federal suicide prevention hotline for LGBTQ youth was defunded. Meanwhile, we know that gender-affirming care is a lifeline for trans youth who suffer from disparate suicide rates—all while their access to health care is increasingly being scaled back or even criminalized.

All this, for existing. All this, for trying to live. This is the very playbook of abusers: punishing someone's attempts at survival.

■ ■ ■

At the same time that President Trump greenlit anti-abortion terrorism targeting doctors and women and cracked down on LGBTQ rights, he also repeatedly claimed to be American women's great "protector" on the campaign trail in 2024. All while a legally recognized sexual abuser himself, Trump claimed he would protect women from the threats of key boogeymen contrived by the fascist imagination: immigrants and trans people.

Throughout 2024 (and, really, for about a decade), he'd campaigned on a pledge to carry out mass deportations and won reelection. Former Vice President Kamala Harris, the Democratic nominee in 2024, inexplicably responded by trying to frame Trump as weak on immigration, pledging to fortify the border further and deport more "criminals" than Trump did in his first term.[15] Their unsettlingly similar approaches reflected a bleak reality: Violent xenophobia is a bipartisan position. And in Congress, Republicans and Democrats spent the better part of 2025 working together on a sweeping agenda to strengthen the mass deportation apparatus by citing faux concerns about women's safety—all as these bills place abuse victims at greater risk.[16]

In the fascist imagination, immigrants are endangering white women. Propagandizing against nonwhite, often Black or brown men as an innate, violent threat to white womanhood is an age-old tactic of white supremacy, historically and presently wielded to facilitate further colonial violence against entire groups. This, of course, is the exact rhetorical strategy that Zionists deploy to demonize Palestinian men and justify genocide, zeroing in on Palestinian men's racial identities and Israeli women's greater relatability and proximity to white, Western audiences. Where immigration policy in the United States is concerned, the lawmakers who present immigrant men as an existential threat to women's safety often pose the greatest threat of all to us, with their abortion restrictions, vile attacks on trans women and queer people, and, of course, their legislation directly targeting immigrants who are victims of abuse and gender-based violence.

In 2025, Congress passed the Laken Riley Act, a law that further harms abuse victims and added fuel to Trump's mass deportation machine—all, horrifically, in the name of a victim of femicide. It was named after a twenty-two-year-old nursing student who was killed in 2024 by an undocumented immigrant man who had previously been charged with shoplifting. The law allows immigrants, including those who legally live and work in the United States, to be indefinitely detained without being charged with a crime—even if they're arrested by mistake. The bill's lack of distinction between legal and undocumented immigrants reminds us that immigrant justice can't be predicated on legality.

A coalition of victim advocates sharply condemned the bill ahead of its passage, accusing it of exploiting their cause to advance xenophobia—all while further harming immigrant survivors. Stephanie Love-Patterson, president of the National Network to End Domestic Violence, warned the Laken Riley Act would make immigrant victims "less likely to seek help from authorities, fearing retaliatory accusations that could lead to detention," consequently "[emboldening] abusers" and "[representing] a step backwards for survivors."[17] The Tahirih Justice Center stressed that the Laken Riley Act's emphasis on petty crimes and shoplifting carries particular harm for domestic violence victims, who are often falsely accused of or forced to commit such crimes under duress from their abusers. Hannah Shapiro, supervising attorney at the DV Immigration Project in New York, said the law "will add real teeth to an abuser's threat to have a survivor arrested and deported as a tool of power and control."[18]

In early 2025, around the same time the Laken Riley Act passed Congress, the House of Representatives passed the heinously named Preventing Violence Against Women by Illegal Aliens Act, or H.R. 30. The bill's lead sponsor, Republican Rep. Nancy Mace from South Carolina, has long wielded "women's safety" as a warped justification for her crusade against trans people. Her bill, H.R. 30, claimed to protect abuse victims by amending the Immigration and Nationality Act so that domestic abusers who are accused of abuse but haven't been convicted of a crime can be deported. But the bill actually renders it exponentially easier for immigrant victims to be deported if they defend themselves against their abusers or are falsely accused of abuse by them. It further broadens the avenues through which immigrant victims, not their abusers, can be deported.[19]

This is fundamentally rooted in DARVO, a highly common and highly successful tactic of abuse. After all, almost a quarter of survivors say that when they called 911 on their abusive partner, they—not their partner—were the ones arrested or threatened with arrest because police officers perceived *them* as the abuser. DARVO is inextricable from xenophobia, which positions immigrants as the abusers and the nation to which they're immigrating as the victim. In many cases, immigrants are forced to flee unsafe, unstable, and sometimes violent conditions—conditions often created by colonizing powers over the course of generations through war, conquest, and exploitation. These same colonizing powers then demonize immigrant populations for migrating and seeking better lives. Xenophobia relies on reversing the victim and offender in this paradigm, portraying immigrants as a unilateral, violent threat to the safety of the "native," white-coded women, and framing the colonizer as a hapless, female-coded victim.

Relatedly, as the Trump administration aggressively attempted to justify the unlawful transfer of Kilmar Abrego Garcia, a legal US resident, to serve a life sentence in a brutal maximum-security prison in El Salvador, the administration's main argument was that Abrego Garcia was an imperfect immigrant with past criminal infractions, so he deserved this outcome. He was an "imperfect victim," so he deserved to rot in a concentration camp. This horrific situation certainly reminds us of Mohammed El-Kurd's assertions in his book *Perfect Victims*—including that "even if" the worst lies and propaganda that a colonizer spins about their victim were true, that wouldn't negate their inalienable human rights. The administration's broader goal amid its attempts to indiscriminately target, detain, and deport immigrants was to frame human rights as conditional based on their criminal records—the same way that abusers defend themselves by framing their victims' rights to safety from violence as conditional based on their behaviors. The administration hyperfocused on weaponizing irrelevant aspects of immigrant men's pasts to frame them as imperfect and thus worthy of deportation and state violence—in the same way that abusers insist that imperfect rape and abuse victims also deserve harm. This is how the administration has treated everyone who is ensnared in its horrific mass deportation operation. One man who was sent to the Salvadoran torture camp was a gay barber who had committed no crimes and was transferred by mistake; he later reported surviving repeated rapes by prison guards.

On the House floor, Mace proudly declared in a graphic, wildly racist rant that she sponsored H.R. 30 "to demonize illegal immigrants who are here raping our women and girls, murdering our women and girls, and who are pedophiles, molesting our children," further baselessly accusing "a horde of illegal aliens" of "molesting American children, battering and bruising and beating up American women, and violently raping American women and girls." To Mace and her base, the fictionalized women and girls in question are white. Mace further advocated for her bill by claiming that "keeping criminal illegal aliens . . . off our streets is just common sense," and "women should be able to walk down the street without fear."[20] Yet, the notion of rape and gender-based violence solely as street-based crimes is right-wing propaganda to bolster support for police. Gender-based violence primarily takes place in the home, perpetrated by partners and acquaintances;[21] the likelihood of its lethality is maximized by state defunding of domestic violence shelters and other resources.

Inflammatory language like this is meant to obscure that the perpetrators of violent crime in this country are overwhelmingly citizens. Divorced from the context of—as Mace put it—"[demonizing] illegal immigrants," xenophobic politicians are entirely uninterested in women's safety. These are often the same people who want guns as accessible as possible, even as seventy women are shot and killed by an intimate partner every month.[22] Their policies defund lifesaving victim services, and their abortion bans fuel rising maternal mortality.[23] They invoke "women's safety" for legislation like this solely to fan the flames of xenophobia and justify significant expansions to the mass deportation apparatus. And liberal, Democratic politicians cynically embrace these policies and narratives to court growing bipartisan support. "The reason the Trump administration and other conservatives use survivors as a shield is because they hope listeners will feel like it's sexist to oppose them," sexual violence researcher Dr. Nicole Bedera told me in 2025.

Republican lawmakers wield this rhetoric about protecting women, "hoping to peel off Democratic support" for their anti-immigrant agenda: "Conservatives aren't particularly interested in protecting women, and they would support deportation on its own. They use this kind of language because they hope we'll join them or begin fighting with each other," Bedera said. "The best thing any of us can do right now is hold firm in our stance that expanding deportation is wrong. The reason doesn't matter. It isn't actually that complicated."

More than 200 immigrant, civil rights, and victim advocacy organizations signed a letter opposing H.R. 30 in 2025, warning that it's more likely to be weaponized against victims who are undocumented. "Language and cultural barriers, fear of the abuser and the authorities, confusion, intimidation, a lack of awareness of rights, and a lack of access to advocates and other resources, all may prevent an immigrant victim from being able to communicate what really happened," the letter stated. "Rather than rushing to enact additional immigration penalties that could cause harm to survivors, we urge Congressional representatives to consult with service providers and survivors themselves to develop legislation that is responsive to their experiences and needs."[24]

If victims commit acts of self-defense, or if their abusers falsely accuse them of abuse, they could face deportation under H.R. 30. Coercive control and false allegations from abusers, which can plunge victims' lives into chaos by implicating them into the criminal or child welfare systems, are everyday occurrences.[25] Abusers often falsely accuse victims of abusing their children, which can criminally implicate them. All of this contributes to the sexual-assault-to-prison pipeline and a prison system in which an estimated 90 percent of incarcerated women have survived sexual violence.

Under H.R. 30, more women could be deported through these same abusive tactics.

Zain Lakhani, director of Migrant Rights and Justice at the Women's Refugee Commission, told *The Intercept* in 2025 that she anticipated that under H.R. 30, if an immigrant survivor is falsely accused and arrested, she could be prompted to sign a no-contest waiver (which accepts penalties without admitting guilt) to be released from jail and reunited with her children. "They may have no idea that this is going to subject them to immigration consequences, but now it's going to subject them to mandatory deportation," Lakhani said.[26]

Even if H.R. 30 functioned as it claimed to, by escalating risk of deportation for abusers, it would *also* discourage many immigrant victims from coming forward. "Survivors feel pressure to protect their abusers, especially if their abusers hold financial power over them or their children," Bedera told me. "In domestic violence, victims' and perpetrators' lives are interconnected. A lot of things intended to hurt a perpetrator will hurt the victim more. This is true even with the best of intentions, but I doubt that conservatives are hoping to protect undocumented survivors. They are openly pushing for collective punishment of entire families."

Historically, we have seen Black and brown men reduced to bestial, often hypersexualized caricatures to justify state violence against them. Colonization, even, is presented as a means to "civilize" them and deny them self-determination that they can't be entrusted with. As I've previously noted, at least 4,743 lynchings occurred in the United States from 1882 to 1968—often by white supremacist vigilantes, enabled by the government. They justified their acts of racial terror and brutality by framing their victims as an innate and immediate physical threat—primarily to white women and girls—just by existing.

We encounter this same, horrific logic applied by the state of Missouri in 2024 to murder Marcellus "Khaliifah" Williams, a Black man who was charged with murdering a white woman, despite serious flaws in the state's case against him, including unreliable witness testimony, lack of forensic evidence, and racial bias in jury selection. As Hannah Greene wrote for *Prism* at the time, "In the cruel imagination of the state, Williams was reduced to the Black brute caricature, preying on helpless white women—nothing but a threat to be destroyed."[27]

We continue to see these tactics—the justification of state violence through the dehumanization of men of color—abroad, where the United States continues to facilitate horrific colonial violence. In Palestine, false allegations of a coordinated mass campaign of sexual violence against Israeli settlers by Hamas fighters serve as a key basis for Israel's genocide. These allegations, peddled by occupation forces and Western media, draw on overtly racist stereotypes about Palestinian and Arab men as barbaric rapists who must be punished, tamed, and controlled and who can't be trusted with freedom and self-determination.

In the United States, the border functions not just as an extension of imperialist, gendered violence, but also as a fundamental act of gendered violence itself. In December 2024, Texas Governor Greg Abbott unveiled a $100,000, state-funded billboard campaign threatening undocumented immigrants with sexual violence if they crossed the border. "How much did you pay to have your daughter raped?" one billboard read. "Your wife and daughter will pay for the trip with their bodies." Another read, "This 14-year-old girl was raped by more than 20 men on her way to the border. Protect your family. Change their fate." We know that between 60 and 80 percent of women and girls face sexual assault crossing the border.[28] In 2018, a Border Patrol official said that he sees migrant girls as young as twelve put on birth control pills "because they know getting violated is part of the journey."[29] Sexual violence committed by immigration authorities is rampant in immigrant detention centers too.[30] All of this is a direct consequence of the United States willfully transforming the border into a militarized zone, shrouding migration in manufactured criminality and violence.

Abbott unveiled the billboards at the time while speaking at a stunt press conference in front of a "rape tree"—a term for notorious locations along the border where immigrant women are raped by traffickers and smugglers. The governor then described his billboards as "tough medicine." He said these messages "implore those people in Central America to consider the violent, horrific realities of what will happen to the women and children they bring with them. . . . We want no more rape trees in Texas. Do not make the dangerous trek to Texas."

The billboard campaign came roughly three years after Abbott personally pledged to "eliminate rape" in order to justify his abortion ban's distinct lack of a rape exception in 2021.

Again, the myth of rape exclusively as a street-based crime is right-wing propaganda to bolster support for police; in reality, rape and gender-based violence primarily take place in the home. But it's not as if any of that matters to Abbott, who exclusively understands rape as a rhetorical tool. Abbott, in any case, most certainly did not "eliminate rape": Researchers estimated in January 2024 that there had been 26,300 rape-induced pregnancies in Texas alone since the *Dobbs* ruling in 2022. Abbott's billboards effectively exposed that Republican politicians *know* their sweeping narrative that those who cross the border are mythologized, violent criminals is a lie. They are instead often incredibly vulnerable individuals—including families, women, and children—typically fleeing horrific circumstances that US policies have exacerbated.

In reality, perpetrators of violent crime in the United States are overwhelmingly citizens.[31] But this is immaterial to anti-immigrant lawmakers because their goal is mass deportations; they're uninterested in splitting hairs about criminality and reality. Their motivation isn't to make any of us safer. Their motivation, rather, is to endanger and remove the targets of their xenophobia, and they're willing to wield any amount of disinformation and vile, racist smears to advance this agenda. Consider, for instance, how Vice President JD Vance in 2024 pushed a range of baseless lies that Haitian immigrant communities in his home state of Ohio were stealing and eating people's cats and dogs. As a result of these lies, several schools and public buildings in Springfield, Ohio, had to be evacuated due to threats of violence galvanized by Vance's rhetoric.[32] In the same breath that xenophobic politicians claim to be motivated by safety, they endanger all of us.

Within months of starting his second term, President Trump, along with congressional Republicans, passed a sweeping budget bill that invested more than $100 billion in ICE and border enforcement.[33] The budget came as ICE agents escalated their campaign of terror on immigrant communities across the United States, especially after Trump rescinded policies that once restricted immigration enforcement in locations like domestic violence shelters, hospitals, and churches. And, predictably enough, civilian men reportedly began impersonating ICE agents to kidnap and sexually assault immigrant women. It's not difficult: They can wear plain clothes, conceal their faces to avoid accountability, and don't need paraphernalia to immediately identify themselves as officers. ICE has even directed its agents to arrest people and enter more people's homes without warrants. The reported stories in the summer of 2025 were horrifying: A North Carolina man posing as ICE threatened to deport an immigrant woman, then kidnapped and raped her; a Maryland man flashed a fake ICE badge, then also kidnapped and raped a woman in his car; a New York man posing as an ICE agent assaulted and tried to rape a woman, before robbing her and fleeing the scene in broad daylight.[34]

Several lawmakers in the California legislature and in Congress introduced legislation to address horrific scenarios like this by requiring ICE agents to have proper identification and prohibiting them from covering their faces. Bills like this could be a step in the right direction. But we can't bury the deeper, driving forces behind why this is happening. This phenomenon is only possible because of the impunity that state agents—ICE agents, police officers, prison staff—have always had to abuse and control women and victims' bodies. Civilians are impersonating state agents to assault vulnerable women and victims, because state agents—under every presidential administration—have always been able to do this. In 2020, a whistleblower revealed that a doctor at an immigrant detainment center had nonconsensually sterilized at least eighteen women; more than forty women testified that they'd been subjected to invasive medical procedures while in ICE custody.[35] As we have seen throughout history, this is by no means a new tactic. The state has previously, systematically inflicted forced sterilizations on Indigenous populations and poor and disabled populations. To this day, incarcerated people are also pressured and sometimes forced to undergo state-mandated sterilizations. The goal is eugenics: the policing and erasure of certain populations that the state deems to be unfit.

"All our lives, we are taught to fear masked men in unmarked vehicles," the House Democratic Women's Caucus wrote in a letter to the Trump administration in 2025. "We learn we should run from such men to avoid being kidnapped, sexually assaulted, or killed. Yet, ICE is increasingly conducting raids and arrests in masks, plainclothes, without visible identification or badges, using unmarked vehicles—tactics that cause confusion, terror, and mistrust among the public."[36]

Again: The only reason civilians began performing as state agents to get away with sexual violence is that across the country, state power in a range of forms is routinely wielded to perpetrate gender-based violence without consequence. Unmasking ICE agents is important, but it's a Band-Aid over a broader, systemic crisis.

Sexual abuse, often inflicted on children, is rampant across immigrant detainment centers. Existing research has indicated 40 percent of police officers self-report committing domestic violence against their spouses or children, and 60 percent of prison rapes are committed by guards and staff. Sexual abuse is the second-most common form of police misconduct.

It wasn't until 2022 that Congress passed the Closing the Law Enforcement Consent Loophole Act, ending a loophole that previously allowed cops to sexually abuse individuals in their custody and defend themselves from charges by claiming the encounter was consensual, which is impossible. From 2006 to 2016, at least 26 of 158 law enforcement officers who were charged with unlawful sexual contact with people they'd arrested invoked the "consent defense."[37]

They were acquitted or had their charges dropped.

Ultimately, men wouldn't be posing as ICE agents and assaulting women if ICE didn't exist at all. The agency's very existence, and the vile policing of immigrants in this nation, dehumanizes immigrants and renders them exponentially more vulnerable to a range of violence, including gender-based violence.

Of course men know that if they pose as the state, they can get away with what the state so often does, which is terrorize and violate women and victims, and especially victims in more precarious positions. ICE must be abolished, and the root causes of state and carceral violence must be addressed.

The state itself is the foremost abuser of women and survivors—all as it hides behind racist caricatures and graphic, anti-immigrant atrocity propaganda. In reality, one of the foremost threats to abuse victims' safety is declining funding for and access to victim services and shelters. Lakhani told me in 2025 that Trump's executive order to rescind the "sensitive zone" status of domestic violence shelters—as well as hospitals, churches, and schools—and allow ICE officers to enter and detain victims could be life-threatening for immigrant abuse victims. Under these circumstances, they'll be unable to leave their abusers and take their children to seek shelter, lest they risk deportation. "Taken together, these and other policies force immigrant survivors into impossible choices between their immediate safety and arrest and deportation," she said. "They also hand a powerful tool for coercion back to abusers."

Mace and other right-wing politicians have deployed similar tactics against trans people, attempting to ban trans women from as many spaces as possible to "protect" cis women, all while giddily electing a serially accused rapist—Trump—president. "Women's safety" is the same warped justification for anti-abortion laws that impose medically unnecessary requirements on clinics to shut them down.

The right-wing gender binary, Bedera told me, is about establishing cis women as victim and cis men as protector. "We lose freedoms every time we're expected to rigidly conform to a gender role, especially since the Trump administration's ideology of gender conformity is patriarchal. In this context, the phrase 'protecting women' really means 'controlling women,'" she explained.

And those who are at the margins—like immigrant survivors—will be among the most vulnerable, all as *they're* framed as the real threats.

7

REVOLUTIONARY VIOLENCE, SELF-DEFENSE, AND MASS ACTION

Bodies fall, not ideas.

—GHASSAN KANAFANI

In 1972 a Swedish journalist asked Angela Davis, just out of prison, if she "approved of violence" by revolutionary activists. "Ask me? If I approve of violence? This does not make any sense," she said.[1] In her 2015 book, *Freedom Is a Constant Struggle*, Davis elaborates further on her part in this iconic exchange, forty-three years later: "Questions about the validity of violence should have been directed to the institutions that held and continue to hold a monopoly on violence: the police, the prisons, the military," she wrote. "At the time, I was in jail, having been falsely charged with murder, kidnapping, and conspiracy, and turned into a target of institutional violence, and I was the one being asked whether I agreed with violence."[2]

Such is often the case: Those without state power are the ones first called on to condemn violence, real or perceived, while the same is never asked of those who wield all power over and commit horrific violence against us, against the masses, on a structural level.

What are and aren't the "right" ways to respond to state violence, to violence from the dominant classes? What are the "right" and "wrong" ways to fight to be free—is there such a thing as a "wrong" way? Is it not self-defense?

■ ■ ■

Across the left, there's an extensive array of positions on political violence, what constitutes violence, and when it is and isn't justified. Case in point: In the summer of 2024, the Communist Party USA condemned the assassination attempt on Donald Trump by a young man with ambiguous but right-leaning politics. "We know only too well the consequence of the assassinations of political figures. As we said many times the CPUSA rejects violence and terror: they only serve the interests of the forces of hate and division," the party said on its website. "Awakening Martin Luther King Jr's dream and tradition of engaging millions in mass protest is the road to real change, peace and progress."[3] In contrast with the US Communist Party in 2024, Davis's perspective on violence is notably more open-minded and cognizant of situational power dynamics. For instance, we know that Trump is responsible for exponentially greater harm rendered against humanity than any individual who would hypothetically harm him. Nonetheless, the US Communist Party's position rejects the notion that this power differential matters, arguing that no amount of violence inflicted by Trump would justify retaliatory violence against him. The different perspectives across leftist organizations and thought leaders signal what strategies an organized left wing might apply to ignite a revolution, and it's striking to take in just how wide-ranging these perspectives are.

■ ■ ■

In Jackie Wang's landmark essay "Against Innocence," she argues that victims of state violence are often introduced to the general public in the context of their criminal behaviors. She points to the case of Isaiah Simmons, a Black teenager who was suffocated to death by five counselors who attacked him in a juvenile detention center: "By emphasizing that it was a juvenile offender who died, the [coverage] immediately flags Simmons as a criminal, signaling to readers that his death is inconsequential and thus not worthy of sympathy." She compares the cultural reaction to Simmons's death with the reaction to the white supremacist vigilante murder of Trayvon Martin in 2012, which sparked national outcry. Predictably enough, right-wing media would eventually find ways to spin and justify Martin's murder. But Wang argues that the mainstream liberal response to Martin's death was one of outrage because he'd been "innocent"—he hadn't attacked the white man who killed him, he was unarmed, he had no criminal record. "Innocence becomes a necessary precondition for the launching of mass anti-racist political campaigns," Wang argues.[4]

In a similar vein, based on how they respond to the violence they face—state violence, or colonial or white supremacist terror, or gender-based violence—some victims are deemed worthy and sympathetic but others are not. If they respond to any of the aforementioned violence, if they resist, if they are traumatized or ill-adjusted as a result of trauma, if their behaviors and responses are designated as criminal, they are no longer "innocent."

Liberal politics craves martyrs—perfect victims, crushed by the system, by an ontologically evil oppressor. Victims who are peaceful and nonviolent until the end, no matter what they're forced to endure. The term "martyr" carries different meanings across different spaces and cultures. In the Arab world, a "martyr" is someone who dies for their faith or a noble cause; throughout Israel's genocidal campaign against Gaza, Palestinians have mourned their dead as martyrs, killed by Israel for daring to live on their own land. Sacrifice is a revolutionary reality.

Fascism, and the dominant institutions and individuals who carry water for fascism, can monopolize on martyrs, too. Wang raises in "Against Innocence" that often enough, the state capitalizes on outrage against individual killings of and acts of violence enacted on "innocent" victims, because it can publicly perform as an ally to protesters by criminalizing and inflicting retribution on the individuals responsible—for example, the "bad" cops who killed George Floyd in 2020 were convicted, pacifying an outraged public, all while the innately fascist and white supremacist institution of policing is allowed to remain intact. The US Congress's response to Floyd's state murder consisted of a spate of "police reform" bills that further invested in policing, paying for additional "trainings" for police and additional surveillance technologies to supposedly monitor cops and hold them accountable, while, in reality, further bolstering the surveillance state writ large.

Is Luigi Mangione, a young man who suffered greatly and appears to have suffered a prolonged mental health episode culminating in the alleged murder of UnitedHealthcare's Brian Thompson, a martyr? Not in the liberal imagination, because he responded to violence with violence.

The consensus about Mangione and his alleged actions, among the left, is broadly sympathetic; there is certainly stratification in whether American leftists agree with his alleged actions, but there is consensus in understanding those actions. There is consensus in understanding that his alleged act of violence was not senseless, that it was a response to a greater, systemic violence.

■ ■ ■

In the United States today, the federal minimum wage hasn't increased since 2009—when it increased to $7.25 per hour. Wages have remained stagnant, far too few US residents can afford to buy a house, every community is being ravaged by climate catastrophes in some way, and "medical debt" is pervasive. Through all of this, billionaires have only consolidated wealth and power, and have further embedded themselves in our government. The wealthiest man in the world held a marketing campaign for his barely functional electric cars on the White House lawn in March 2025.[5] Capitalists tell us that our lives are bad not because of their greed, but because of the very existence of our most vulnerable and marginalized neighbors—immigrants and trans people, for instance.

Leftist movements understand that our lives will never improve without solidarity, without seeing ourselves in each other, and, consequently, becoming immune to fascist, capitalist propaganda that upholds the status quo by obscuring who is responsible for the world's suffering. There is more than enough for everyone—but sacrifices will ultimately be required of many of us before our conditions improve on a systematic level.

In many ways, these ideals reflect the legacy of the Marxist-Leninist revolutionary Che Guevara, whose military leadership and thought leadership alike remain as prescient as ever as American leftists today find ourselves at an inflection point in history.

In the years after Guevara and Fidel Castro's revolutionary takeover of Cuba in 1959, while Castro governed, Guevara traveled and convened with oppressed people of the world, seeking to galvanize them to take up arms and resist their colonizers. "Guevarism" emerged as a powerful theory of communist revolution through guerrilla warfare. Guevara further envisioned that revolution and liberation through armed struggle would produce a new type of human being, or a "new man": someone who was committed to the collective good and willing and eager to sacrifice—even himself—to this cause. At the core of Guevara's politics was the belief that, contrary to liberal notions of civility at all costs, violence is not inherently wrong, but is often enough a legitimate means of defense and resistance to oppressive systems, systems that instigate and create the conditions for violence.

He wrote in 1963, "Violence is not the monopoly of the exploiters and as such the exploited can use it too and, moreover, ought to use it when the moment arrives."[6] In his 1961 book, *Guerrilla*

Warfare, Guevara wrote, "We must come to the inevitable conclusion that the guerrilla fighter is a social reformer, that he takes up arms responding to the angry protest of the people against their oppressors, and that he fights in order to change the social system that keeps all his unarmed brothers in ignominy and misery."[7]

In the same text, he characterizes guerrilla warfare as "a war of the masses, a war of the people," explaining:

> The guerrilla band is an armed nucleus, the fighting vanguard of the people. It draws its great force from the mass of the people themselves. The guerrilla band is not to be considered inferior to the army against which it fights simply because it is inferior in firepower. Guerrilla warfare is used by the side which is supported by a majority but which possesses a much smaller number of arms for use in defense against oppression.

At the core of revolutionary violence, Guevara argues, is "tenderness"—it is solidarity and a sincere motivation to alleviate human suffering. Under this thinking, revolutionary violence is a necessary tool to help and uplift the oppressed, to shield and free them from state and colonial violence. For many of us, our longing to see the current world order burn down, our hatred of capitalists and white supremacist institutions, is rooted deeply in love and a desire for human dignity for all. During his 2020 presidential bid, Bernie Sanders, one of the only leftist politicians to excel in mainstream US politics throughout history, asked his supporters, "Are you willing to fight for someone you don't know?" The answer to this question, as the success of his campaign suggests, was overwhelmingly "yes." Many of us *are* willing to fight for someone we don't know—all the more so as we are radicalized to understand that no matter our identity-based differences, our fates are intertwined. That's precisely why right-wing actors work so diligently to sow hatred and division between us: because they fear what could become possible when the workers of the world unite.

■ ■ ■

"People usually fight for something and they stop fighting for something—in Palestinians' case, to liberate [their] country, to have dignity, to have respect, to have [their] mere human rights," Ghassan Kanafani, the Palestinian novelist, journalist, and militant with the Popular Front for the Liberation of Palestine (PFLP), said in 1970.[8] One year earlier, Kanafani drafted the PFLP's 1969 platform, transitioning the party's alignment from pan-Arab nationalism to revolutionary Marxism. Kanafani subscribed to the Leninist definition of imperialism; that is, he understood that it was not just the Israeli regime but Western colonialism writ large that drove the dispossession and displacement of Palestinians. The Palestinian struggle was and is a global struggle shared with the oppressed people of the world. Decades later, in 2022, the pro-Palestine organization Jewish Voice for Peace wrote of Kanafani, "Ghassan Kanafani reminds us there is no symmetry in the amount of, reasons behind, or culpability for violence between 'a colonialist case and a national liberation movement.'"[9]

"You don't ask a man who is being slaughtered, 'What do you think of nonviolence?'" Kanafani said in the final years before he and his young niece were assassinated by Israel. Advocating Peace, a nonprofit for Palestinian human rights, invoked this quote from Kanafani and wrote in July 2025 that, with his writing and activism, he "exposed how the West demanded that Palestinians remain 'civil' in the face of tanks, drones, land theft, and military occupation. . . . This biting indictment of liberal double standards still resonates today. Western media and politicians continue to excuse Israel's genocidal violence while branding Palestinian resistance as 'terrorism.' Kanafani's work challenges us to ask: Who gets to resist? And who decides what resistance looks like?"

An Israeli journalist, Danny Rubinstein, sympathized with Kanafani in his Hebrew biography of Kanafani written in 2022, in which Rubinstein argues that violent resistance from Palestinians was a reasonable response to Zionist violence and colonialism. "Israel destines Palestinians to a life of permanent imprisonment, whether it is the prison of exile or the prison of living under an apartheid regime. Kanafani's vision defies this Israeli aspiration," Rubinstein wrote.[10]

In the summer of 2025, we began to see a shift in public consensus. In neoliberal spaces that for so long unequivocally backed Israel, we encountered growing sympathy toward Palestinians as mass starvation took hold of Gaza and the images and horrors on the ground became increasingly impossible for Israel to conceal. Still, Zionists doubled down. They either engaged in a strain of Holocaust denial and denied the truth that we all saw before us—or they retorted that these realities were a necessity in response to the events of October 7, 2023.

When Zionists insinuate that Israel had a right to respond to October 7, 2023, with genocide, "the implication [is] that Palestine was supposed to do nothing after decades of colonial violence," Palestinian American lawyer and writer Dylan Saba wrote.[11] Similarly, as mentioned earlier in this book, Palestinian writer Mohammed El-Kurd has pointed out that such colonial violence is frequently not regarded as violence, but rather "as management, bureaucracy, a necessary fact of life."

In September 2025, the Gaza Health Ministry reported that nearly 500 people—mostly children—had starved to death since October 2023 while more than 320,000 children under the age of five in Gaza were at imminent risk of acute malnutrition. Tens of thousands more Palestinians in Gaza suffered from the most severe and deadliest form of undernutrition. In the imperialist imagination, policy—imposing a deadly blockade on Gaza, torturing to death hundreds of thousands of children via starvation, all while continuing to bomb, maim, and shoot at the captive population—is not violent; Hamas guerrilla fighters responding to colonization are.

"Bodies fall, not ideas" is, today, one of Kanafani's most iconic and prescient quotes. It is impossible to quantify how many lives Zionism has already destroyed and impossible to predict how many more it will destroy. But what can't be destroyed is the revolutionary idea that Palestine must and will be free—whatever it may take.

■ ■ ■

The murder of the UnitedHealthcare CEO came as a shock, yet, at the same time, it wasn't surprising; it was, in some ways, the natural conclusion of a society at the end of its rope. No one likes the US health insurance model—in a country where you'd struggle to find consensus that the sun is hot, nearly everyone across the political spectrum can agree that the system is dehumanizing, inefficient, and, of course, making nearly all of us sicker. Despite this, nothing ever changes: A lone US senator here and there might introduce a "health care for all" bill that lives and dies in committee, or a law like the Affordable Care Act, introducing small, moderate changes, might narrowly pass. Under the ACA, health care remains impossible to access for large swaths of the country—yet, the ACA, still, went too far for right-wing lawmakers who are constantly attacking it, with minimal pushback from their liberal opponents.

More than 100 years before the murder of Brian Thompson, in 1911, Russian revolutionary Leon Trotsky wrote the essay "Why Marxists Oppose Individual Terrorism."[12]

"Our class enemies are in the habit of complaining about our terrorism. What they mean by this is rather unclear," he begins. "They would like to label all the activities of the proletariat directed against the class enemy's interests as terrorism." He argued that "the entire class struggle is nothing but terrorism" to the ruling class.

To that end, he opposed acts of violence like the slaying of Brian Thompson. He argued that such attacks "belittle" the masses and encourage us to wait for and bend the knee to individual saviors. The revolution, he argued, should be rooted in mass action, solidarity, and consensus rather than individual acts:

> Only the conscious and organised working class can send a strong representation into the halls of parliament to look out for proletarian interests. However, in order to murder a prominent official you need not have the organised masses behind you. . . .
>
> If it makes sense to terrify highly placed personages with the roar of explosions, where is the need for the party? Why meetings, mass agitation and elections if one can so easily take aim at the ministerial bench from the gallery of parliament? . . .
>
> In our eyes, individual terror is inadmissible precisely because it belittles the role of the masses in their own consciousness, reconciles them to their powerlessness, and turns their eyes and hopes towards a great avenger and liberator who some day will come and accomplish his mission.

"If we oppose terrorist acts," he concludes, "it is only because individual revenge does not satisfy us."

In a similar vein, the Venezuelan American activist Peter Camejo argued against both liberalism and "ultraleftism."[13] Ultraleftists believe the ruling class is ontologically evil and holds all power, in contrast with liberals, who believe they can create all necessary change through electing this Democrat or that, even when these Democrats are themselves committed to the status quo of capitalist oppression. Ultraleftists believe capitalist elites hold all power and the masses hold none; consequently, Camejo posits that their theories of change are rooted in small minorities or individual saviors taking extreme, often violent actions to force concessions from elites or drive elites out of power. These extreme actions include riots, terror, and armed revolution. Ultraleftists have "given up on the masses," Camejo argued in a 1970 speech. "The actions they propose are not aimed at the American people," Camejo said. "They're aimed at those who have already radicalized. They know beforehand that masses of people won't respond to the tactics they propose."

Drawing on Camejo's language about ultraleftists, Young Democratic Socialists of America's Lex Von Klark wrote in 2021:

> This disbelief in the power of the masses also leads them to denounce many mass-strategies as "insufficiently radical," claiming that they have been co-opted and are actually tools of the elites. As Camejo says, ultraleftists represent a small portion of the broader left, but make up a significant proportion of those who consider themselves radicals or socialists. They are extremely common on the Internet, as thousands of newly disillusioned liberals have taken up radical aesthetics over the past few years and joined communities of like-minded ultraleftists who encourage each other's increasing immersion in the subculture—thus increasing their distance from the real state of society outside their bubble.[14]

Camejo consequently argued that mass action is the solution. Liberalism and ultraleftism both betray the masses by overly or exclusively orienting around the ruling class—for liberals, that looks like a near-exclusive focus on electing specific liberal representatives, whereas, for ultraleftists, that looks like praying that a few individual actions will spontaneously lead to a crusade of revolutionary violence and assassinations. Mass action, meanwhile, mobilizes workers who hold vastly greater strength in numbers than the ruling class to use those numbers and use class consciousness to create change.

"This is the concept of getting people into motion, into action . . . organizing actions which are able to give expression to the mass opposition to the policies of the ruling class, at the level of understanding that people have reached about what's happening in this society," Camejo said in 1970. "It's the concept of bringing masses into motion, but at all times keeping the movement independent of the ruling class." He continued:

> Now, what is the best way we can implement this orientation at this point? We follow a general organizational type strategy which is simply this. You get the issues around which people are moving against the government and create a unified movement around them, in order to maximize the numbers that will come into motion. . . .
>
> This is the same strategy which is used by a union when it carries out a strike. When a union calls a strike, it calls it on certain demands. Higher pay, better working conditions, whatever the demands happen to be for that struggle. If a majority of the workers agree, they take a vote, and then everybody strikes together, and they put a very heavy emphasis on keeping it together.

Mass political education, unity, and community care and solidarity, Camejo argues, are the most sustainable and effective responses to state violence. That's probably why right-wing propaganda, mass disinformation campaigns, and the destruction of credible journalism—even a credible reality—proliferate under fascism. Consider the acceleration of artificial intelligence technologies imposed on us as our inevitable future. AI and the rising tide of fascism are vastly connected. AI is a massive force toward misinformation and disempowering workers by threatening their employment; fascism relies on both.[15] AI deepens inequality by plagiarizing and stealing from artists, writers, and academics to further enrich billionaires and capitalists, all while simultaneously cheapening labor and granting capitalists exponentially greater power over our lives and the information—the reality, really—that we have access to.

The state is far more militarized than it has ever been. We live in a surveillance state that has rendered the organizing and strategizing that acts of revolutionary violence require increasingly difficult if not impossible. Drones and new, advanced weapons and military technology have rendered the state increasingly impermeable to acts of violent resistance that might have been possible even a few decades ago. If we're all waiting for someone to "do it" (that is, assassinate the fascist President Donald Trump, or assassinate any number of other fascist government officials now or in the future), to free us, to incite the revolution while we simply continue with our day-to-day lives uninterrupted until then, that is, as Camejo suggests, certainly a good way to justify doing nothing.

■ ■ ■

In writing this, my goal was not to be prescriptive, to map a single clear path forward, or provide the one single correct answer to how to topple evil regimes and achieve collective liberation. Rather, I wanted to present a short history of theories of revolutionary violence and analyze its historic and ongoing function as self-defense. Instead of a prescription, I wanted this to be a sampling of perspectives from different scholars, activists, and movement leaders about revolutionary violence and mass action.

But I approach this conversation, as I approach all conversations about state violence and resistance, from the perspective of a survivor of sexual violence and someone whose research and expertise focus on gender-based violence, abuse, and domination. On a personal level, I don't condemn self-defense and I refuse to see violence from oppressed people, violence from abuse victims, violence from the colonized in service of trying to be free, in a silo; I don't condemn anyone who tries to be free or responds to state violence. Of course, whether these methods present the most viable and effective path forward to overturning imperialist power structures, I can't say with any certainty.

At the same time, I hold a less harsh and cynical view of "ultra-leftists" than Camejo might have. Many are right to be disillusioned and disempowered under the current paradigm, for one thing. And for another, violent acts are not without some degree of utility. Fear is a natural deterrent; in a just world, oppressors, capitalists, agents of state and imperialist violence, should not be able to operate, to enact mass violence and profiteer in mass death, without living in fear for their lives. Fear of punishment and retaliation are arguably a fair hazard of industry for being a health insurance CEO or a fascist.

Is revolutionary violence valid self-defense? While I argue that it is, that can be true at the same time that it is not the only way forward.

8

CONCLUSION

In November 2024, the immediate aftermath of Donald Trump's reelection gave way to a particularly vicious cycle of cyberharassment perpetrated by male, pro-Trump trolls. They rallied around the slogan "your body, my choice," slinging it at mostly young women and feminists in comment sections, on social media, even in elementary schools and in the streets.[1] This tagline seemed to serve as smug double entendre—inseparable from Trump's election, from his party's support for a national abortion ban, is his status as a legally recognized sexual abuser and serially accused assailant. "Your body, my choice" says the quiet part aloud: Abortion bans are rape; abortion bans are gender-based violence and subjugation. *Your body, my choice.* Abortion bans put abusive men in charge of our bodies.

The day after Election Day in 2024, calls to the Trevor Project's crisis services hotline for LGBTQ youth surged by 200 percent.[2] Online searches for abortion pills and emergency contraception skyrocketed, too.[3] Queer youth, women, and girls were clearly concerned about what a second Trump presidency meant for their safety and their futures. But instead of considering their fears, we were implicitly and explicitly called on to consider the forces that had seemingly pushed large swaths of young men further to the right. This was largely attributed to the online manosphere—a cult of male influencers that often reel in young men by creating seemingly apolitical content about weight lifting, video games, MMA fighting, and dating advice.[4] These interests are rapidly wielded as a pipeline to inundate young men with out-of-context stats and arguments about how much easier it is for women to get jobs, or minorities to get into college, or trans people to succeed at sports. These audiences are radicalized to believe a liberal, feminist world order is crushing them, but electing hypermasculine fascists like Donald Trump can restore young men's access to traditional, patriarchal power—by punishing women, queer people, people of color, and other marginalized classes of people and putting them back in their places.

The rights of women, LGBTQ people, and immigrants have been eroding for years, but TikTok and YouTube videos that amass billions of views have completely buried this reality, instead convincing young men that they're the real victims. "Let's say one of their listeners doesn't get the job or get into the school they want—they'll connect that to what someone like Andrew Tate is telling them about how much easier it is to get a job when you're a woman," Angelo Carusone, president of Media Matters for America, told me in 2024. Tate, if you're lucky enough to be unaware, is an alleged serial rapist, abuser, and human trafficker who built a massive following from instructing young men on how to become "alphas." Key lessons from Tate, for instance, include how to beat and physically harm women, and how to manipulate, exploit, and traffic them for money.

As a reporter writing about topics like violence against women, political disinformation, and MeToo and anti-MeToo backlash for the last several years, a lot of this—particularly figures like Tate—is familiar to me. I remember coming of age during the first Trump administration and being told that young people would follow the lead of voices like climate activist Greta Thunberg or the Parkland school shooting survivors and save the world. Instead, in 2022, I watched large swaths of Gen Z use their social media accounts to mock and harass Amber Heard during her domestic violence defamation trial in a cultural phenomenon that one media scholar labeled "a public orgy of misogyny."[5]

In the ensuing days after the 2024 election, Democrats convened yet another iteration of post-annihilation soul-searching, and many were swift to blame the party's messaging. Bernie Sanders pointed to the party's neglect of the working class but also blamed its supposed embrace of "identity politics." The neoliberal Congressman Mondaire Jones, who lost his House seat the prior election cycle, called on Democrats to cater to right-wing fearmongering about the border. And Rep. Seth Moulton, a prominent Massachusetts Democrat, cruelly suggested Democrats lost because they need to acknowledge that trans kids playing sports is scary. (It's not.) In effect, the most marginalized classes who would be most harmed by the electoral outcome, a product of large swaths of white and male voters' hatred and bigotry, were the ones being blamed for that bigotry.[6]

Much of the 2024 election seemed deeply rooted in backlash and retaliation against marginalized identity groups for gaining a modicum of rights and greater cultural representation over the previous decade, allowing white supremacists and misogynists to play victim. Conservative influencers repeatedly catered to this utterly delusional worldview, steering voters to Trump, their protector, who would protect them by putting their "abusers"—women and people of color—back in their place as victims. And, all the while, Democrats were uninterested in meaningfully fighting back, in meaningfully standing up for pregnant people, for immigrants, for trans people. Instead, they tirelessly worked to find common ground with fascists and white supremacists. But in reality, fascists will smear anything even a hair short of fascism as "radical."

About two months before the election, I had an abortion. The outcome of the election felt ineffably personal and devastating. I say that not because electing a Democratic president would have solved the generational crisis unfolding before all of us, but because the psychic toll of being a survivor of sexual violence, of having had abortions, made the reality of a violent man seizing full political control of my body feel unthinkable.

Yet, in the imagination of Trump supporters, abortion bans, state violence against women, all of it, are essential—they're about reclaiming power by overcoming male victimhood, which they have deemed to be an innate product of feminism. Male victimhood occurs when men are denied total hegemony over women's bodies and lives, when women no longer have to rely on men for economic stability and are therefore less accessible and pliable. *That* is male victimhood. And the supposed crisis of male victimhood, men's rights activists argue, can be rectified only through patriarchal state violence.

■ ■ ■

Oppressive institutions' performance of powerlessness and victimhood, and their propagandistic misrepresentations of underclasses who resist them as the real oppressors, are a defining feature of how they maintain power. We encounter this time and again: in the United States' and Israel's justifications for Israel's brutal, endless war on Palestine; in the American criminal legal system's endless violence against survivors; in the right-wing wars on pregnant people, immigrants, and queer and trans people; in how the capitalist class and the state frame resistance and revolutionary violence as isolated and irrational.

Meanwhile, those most harmed by these intersecting, oppressive systems and institutions are often victims of not just state violence, but gender-based violence: Palestinian political prisoners—of all genders and ages—who are subjected to brutal sexual violence by their occupiers and wardens; undocumented immigrants who are facing trafficking and domestic abuse, but can't seek help lest they face detainment and deportation; rape victims who are further harmed by the state, forced to pay thousands out of pocket for medical care under the for-profit health care system, as well as rape victims who are then re-violated by abortion bans.

And in the face of this endemic violence and dehumanization, we are dehumanized further by the state's demand that we do nothing, that we fall in line, that we perform civility. We are dehumanized by its assertion that we are the ones being uncivil and violent if we respond to our conditions and demand better.

In 2022, when the Supreme Court overturned the federal right to abortion, mass protests unfolded. Some activists demonstrated outside Supreme Court justices' homes. Congress acted quickly—not to restore our reproductive rights or protect our humanity, but to protect the safety of the justices.

To state the obvious, the politicians who are eliminating our human rights do not deserve a single moment's peace. If you believe confronting public officials about the material consequences of their dehumanizing policies is "violent," but the government forcing people to be pregnant isn't, you value the status quo and state agents' comfort over your own life. Peaceful protest is, if anything, a gentle, levelheaded response, considering the responses that would actually be proportional to government officials declaring total war on our bodies and lives.

Those who protested outside the justices' homes were particularly chided for violating their privacy. But it was nothing if not ironic to suggest that anti-abortion justices deserve the very protections from protesters that they denied to us. Abortion patients and providers are endangered, harassed, and physically harmed by protesters on a daily basis. Consider, for instance, the 2014 decision *McCullen v. Coakley*, which struck down clinics' right to maintain buffer zones to protect from anti-abortion protesters. And speaking of dangerous protesters who disregard "privacy": Since 1977, there have been at least eleven murders and twenty-six attempted murders of abortion providers, not to mention forty-two bombings of clinics and homes, 194 incidents of arson, and routine stalking, doxing, and threats.[7] In the face of all of this, we're told that the real problem is noisy, angry grandmas stepping on Brett Kavanaugh's lawn.

Additionally, several location data firms have been caught selling or exposing the data of people who go to abortion clinics for as cheap as $160.[8] Anti-abortion organizations frequently traffic in collecting and circulating our private health data with state agencies; at least one state health director has tracked Planned Parenthood patients' menstrual cycles on a literal spreadsheet. Almost every state and the District of Columbia require some form of reporting abortions to the state;[9] fetal burial laws require people to get death certificates for aborted fetuses, entering their abortions into the public record. For years now, right-wing lawmakers have tried to pass legislation to force some of us to personally ask our employers if we want birth control covered in our employee health insurance plans. Legal experts have said the overturn of *Roe* effectively opened the door for the end of same-sex marriage, even the literal policing of sex positions.[10]

The Supreme Court—the state itself, really—is quite literally in our bedrooms and our uteruses. But the real problem, we're told, is that protesters are making Brett Kavanaugh and Clarence Thomas, two men accused of egregious sexual misconduct, uncomfortable. The real problem, we were told in May of 2022, was that someone violated the Supreme Court's privacy by leaking the draft *Dobbs v. Jackson Women's Health* opinion—that is the crime that the FBI was directed to investigate, not the relegation of women and pregnancy-capable people to second-class citizens.

It's not just privacy—those who are outraged by protests against state agents fundamentally misunderstand what violence is, at its core. Violence is children going to bed hungry in a country that refuses to appropriately tax billionaires. Violence is a higher education system so wildly unaffordable that predominantly poor people of color have no other viable options but to enlist in the US military, into which the United States pours $1 trillion each year.[11] And violence is certainly the highest maternal mortality rate among wealthy nations.

To roll over and accept all of this, as we are directed to do, even by those who claim to be our allies, isn't just unthinkable—for so many, it's a death sentence.

■ ■ ■

With this book, I can do little in the way of prescribing solutions or offering up clear next steps. There are a great many people performing all kinds of vital work to resist the seemingly omnipresent evils of our society—there are abortion funds that meet struggling abortion seekers where they are and help them; domestic violence hotlines and shelters that save women's and children's lives; immigration law firms that work tirelessly for families separated by the state; activists who run for local office to create direct change in their communities; and humanitarian workers operating without a fraction of the funding that the United States sends to Israel, who are putting their own lives at risk to save as many Palestinian lives as they can. There is something for everyone to do.

Similarly, the broader fight to challenge, to slow down, and to someday eradicate state violence, to liberate all the world's oppressed people from the abuses of white supremacy, colonialism, and capitalism, follows no single, specific path. The battle plans of different leftist movements are sometimes at odds, sometimes in flux, sometimes bogged down by internal rather than external fights. And I lack the prescriptive lens necessary to take a position on the best way forward.

But I do know that awareness of the oppressor's strategies is a necessary first step—the first step that any viable path forward naturally stems from. Che Guevara argues in *Guerrilla Warfare* that "the first thing to be considered is the adjusting of guerrilla action to the action of the enemy." He called on guerrilla fighters to be well versed in the strengths and weaknesses of the oppressor, to learn quickly, and to adapt and be fluid based on what they learn.[12]

Our oppressors rely on playing victim; time and again, this has been their de facto strategy—to co-opt the playbook of abusers, to victimize large swaths of the world ad infinitum, then portray their own victims as the abuser to justify escalating their own brutality. But this playbook also serves another purpose: It stratifies and creates disunity among the oppressed. It convinces the victims, the marginalized, that some forms of resistance and some demands are too extreme, that the oppressors must be pitied, that with the exception of minor, cosmetic changes, the status quo must remain intact lest victims go too far and become the abusers themselves.

All of our abusers, all abusive entities and perpetrators of state and imperialist violence, play victim. For too long, this strategy has gone unnoticed, unnamed, unchallenged. And this strategy has allowed our abusers to thrive, to launder their violence and brutality as sensible, warranted, to crush resistance beneath an iron fist by framing dissidents as senseless and bent on violence for the sake of violence, not freedom and dignity.

With this book, I've named and identified that strategy, hopefully as a meaningful first step toward challenging it.

Our futures are all intertwined. And the more we collectively resist and dispel propaganda that portrays powerful, abusive institutions as hapless victims, propaganda that attempts to instead turn us against each other, the more of our power we can begin to reclaim.

ACKNOWLEDGMENTS

Foremost, I want to thank the incredible humanitarian organizations and health care workers who guided my reporting on the reproductive health crisis in Gaza amid Israel's genocidal war on the region. Thank you to the Palestinian Family Planning and Protection Association, Medical Aid for Palestinians, UNICEF, the World Health Organization, International Planned Parenthood Federation, and CARE International—for the lifesaving work you perform each day with such sparing resources, and for the time your experts and health care workers took to inform my work. Thank you to the Palestinian journalists who were forced to risk everything to ensure the world couldn't turn a blind eye to genocide. Palestine will be free, and the world owes a profound debt to you for your courage in the face of the unthinkable.

I also want to name and thank some of the fearless experts, activists, and movement journalists to whom I am forever indebted for your expertise, bravery, and endless generosity with your time. In particular: Thank you to Dr. Nicole Bedera and Kat Tenbarge. This book would not exist if it weren't for your brilliant research and reporting, and, above all, our hours of conversations about gender-based violence and how to build a world where it is unthinkable.

And, of course: I want to thank my editor Shayna Keyles and the entire team at North Atlantic Books for your trust, patience, and support for this project. I am constantly learning so much from all of you, and I'm deeply inspired by how profoundly you care for your authors and the stories we have come together to tell. I was twenty years old when we first started working together, and none of what I have done since would have been possible without our first collaboration. Thank you.

To my friends and family: You know how much I love you. And to survivors all over the world: Like each of my books before, this one is for you. Everything I do, I hope, is an act toward building the world that I truly believe we deserve.

NOTES

INTRODUCTION

1 Jennifer J. Freyd, "II. Violations of Power, Adaptive Blindness and Betrayal Trauma Theory" (PDF), *Feminism & Psychology* 7, no. 1 (February 1997): 22–32, https://doi.org/10.1177/0959353597071004.

2 Sarah J. Harsey, Alexis A. Adams-Clark, and Jennifer J. Freyd, "Associations Between Defensive Victim-Blaming Responses (DARVO), Rape Myth Acceptance, and Sexual Harassment," *PLOS One* 19, no. 12 (December 4, 2024), https://doi.org/10.1371/journal.pone.0313642.

3 Jeremy Diamond, "Trump Says It's 'a Very Scary Time for Young Men in America,'" CNN, October 2, 2018, www.cnn.com/2018/10/02/politics/trump-scary-time-for-young-men-metoo.

4 Sarah Nesbitt and Sage Carson, "The Cost of Reporting: Perpetrator Retaliation, Institutional Betrayal, and Student Survivor Pushout," Advocates for Youth, 2021, www.advocatesforyouth.org/resources/the-cost-of-reporting-perpetrator-retaliation-institutional-betrayal-and-student-survivor-pushout/.

5 Kylie Cheung, "Jonathan Majors' Trial Has Been Jarring. Domestic Violence Experts Have Seen It All Before," *Jezebel*, December 15, 2023, www.jezebel.com/jonathan-majors-trial-has-been-jarring-domestic-violence-experts-have-seen-it-all-before.

6 United Nations Human Rights Office, "Update Report: Six-Month Update Report on the Human Rights Situation in Gaza: 1 November 2023 to 30 April 2024," November 8, 2024, www.ohchr.org/sites/default/files/documents/countries/opt/20241106-Gaza-Update-Report-OPT.pdf.

7 Save the Children, "Gaza: More than 10 Children a Day Lose a Limb in Three Months of Brutal Conflict," January 7, 2024, www.savethechildren.net/news/gaza-more-10-children-day-lose-limb-three-months-brutal-conflict.

8 Antony Loewenstein, *The Palestine Laboratory: How Israel Exports the Technology of Occupation Around the World* (Verso Books, 2023).

9 Dania Akkad, "Israeli Soldiers Have Been Sexually Assaulting Palestinian Women for Decades. Now They're Speaking Out," *Middle East Eye*, December 3, 2024, www.middleeasteye.net/news/israel-sexual-assault-palestinian-women.

10 Kylie Cheung, "In Gaza, the Gender-Based Violence Against Palestinians 'Can Only Be Described as Systematic,'" *Jezebel*, March 24, 2025, www.jezebel.com/in-gaza-the-gender-based-violence-against-palestinians-can-only-be-described-as-systematic.
11 Katherine Hearst, "Israel-Palestine War: Israel Shut Down NGO for Reporting Rape of Teenager, Ex-US Official Says," *Middle East Eye*, December 5, 2023, www.middleeasteye.net/news/israel-palestine-war-ngo-shut-down-reporting-sexual-assault-ex-us.
12 "Israel-Hamas War: Biden Condemns Rapes by Hamas on Oct. 7 and Its Refusal to Release Remaining Women," *New York Times*, December 5, 2023, www.nytimes.com/live/2023/12/05/world/israel-hamas-war-gaza-news.
13 Nicholas Wu, "Jayapal Denies Resolution Condemning Hamas' Sexual Violence Is Related to Her Comments," *Politico*, December 5, 2023, www.politico.com/live-updates/2023/12/05/congress/jayapal-responds-to-hamas-resolution-00130196.
14 Maggie Severns, "Biden Defiant as Democrats Unleash Barrage of Criticism," *Politico*, June 20, 2019.
15 Kat Tenbarge, "Kilmar Abrego Garcia and the Myth of the Perfect Victim," Spitfire News, April 21, 2025, https://spitfirenews.com/p/kilmar-abrego-garcia-myth-perfect-victim.

CHAPTER 1

1 Richard Carleton interview of Ghassan Kanafani, Beirut, October 16, 1970, YouTube, www.youtube.com/watch?v=pRXPImNyMXM.
2 *Time*, "Middle East: Death of a Guerrilla," July 24, 1972, https://time.com/archive/6839986/middle-east-death-of-a-guerrilla/.
3 Kylie Cheung, *Survivor Injustice: State-Sanctioned Abuse, Domestic Violence, and the Fight for Bodily Autonomy* (North Atlantic Books, 2023).
4 Nicole Bedera, *On the Wrong Side: How Universities Protect Perpetrators and Betray Survivors of Sexual Violence* (University of California Press, 2024).
5 *VICE News*, "How Hamas' Leader in Gaza Reacted to the Ceasefire," June 2, 2021, YouTube, www.youtube.com/watch?v=1Px6AyVjw2A&pp=ygUWdmljZSBuZXdzIHlhaHlhIHNpbndhcg%3D%3D.
6 Francesca Borri, "Hamas Leader Sinwar: 'I Don't Want Any More Wars,'" Ynet Global, October 3, 2018, www.ynetnews.com/article/5363595.
7 US Senate Foreign Relations Committee, "Senate Republicans Block Iron Dome Funding," October 4, 2021, www.foreign.senate.gov/press/dem/release/senate-republicans-block-iron-dome-funding.
8 Dylan Saba, "Iron Dome Is Not a Defensive System," *Jewish Currents*, May 25, 2023, https://jewishcurrents.org/iron-dome-is-not-a-defensive-system.

9 Mary Turfah, "Israel's Reality Principle," *Parapraxis*, September 15, 2024, www.parapraxismagazine.com/articles/israels-reality-principle.

10 Rasha Khatib, Martin McKee, and Salim Yusuf, "Counting the Dead in Gaza: Difficult but Essential," *Lancet* 404, no. 10449 (July 20, 2024): 237–238, https://doi.org/10.1016/s0140-6736(24)01169-3.

11 Isaac Chotiner, "The War on Gaza's Children," *New Yorker*, July 7, 2025, www.newyorker.com/news/q-and-a/the-war-on-gazas-children.

12 Jonah Valdez, "Gaza Humanitarian Foundation Head Boasts Success as Palestinians Starve," *Intercept*, July 24, 2025, https://theintercept.com/2025/07/24/gaza-humanitarian-foundation-israel-aid-starvation/.

13 Al Jazeera, "What Is Hamas? A Simple Guide to the Armed Palestinian Group," October 16, 2025, www.aljazeera.com/news/2023/10/8/what-is-the-group-hamas-a-simple-guide-tothe-palestinian-group.

14 Emanuel Fabian, "Defense Minister Announces 'Complete Siege' of Gaza: No Power, Food or Fuel," *Times of Israel*, October 9, 2023, www.timesofisrael.com/liveblog_entry/defense-minister-announces-complete-siege-of-gaza-no-power-food-or-fuel/.

15 Malak A. Tantesh, Lorenzo Tondo, and Julian Borger, "Evidence of 'Execution-Style' Killings of Palestinian Aid Workers by Israeli Forces, Doctor Says," *Guardian*, April 2, 2025, www.theguardian.com/world/2025/apr/02/evidence-execution-style-killings-palestinian-workers-israeli-forces-doctor-says.

16 Alice Cuddy, "Chemical Burns, Assaults, Electric Shocks—Gazans Tell BBC of Torture in Israeli Detention," BBC, April 7, 2025, www.bbc.com/news/articles/cn7vje365rno.

17 Kylie Cheung, "U.S. Doctors Back from Gaza Say the DNC Speeches, Rhetoric Feel Like an Alternate Reality," *Jezebel*, August 20, 2024, www.jezebel.com/american-doctors-back-from-gaza-say-the-dnc-speeches-rhetoric-feel-like-an-alternate-reality.

18 Mehul Srivastava and James Shotter, "The Year That Changed Israel," *Financial Times*, October 6, 2024, www.ft.com/content/f05f0472-a51f-4c26-aadf-08ab7df9e8b3.

19 *Haaretz*, "WATCH: 'We Can Never Forgive the Arabs for Making Us Kill Children'—CBS' Schieffer Quotes Golda Meir," July 28, 2014, www.haaretz.com/israel-news/2014-07-28/ty-article/we-can-never-forgive-them/0000017f-e587-da9b-a1ff-edefe0bd0000.

20 Kylie Cheung, "'On Trial for Crimes Committed Against You': Mohammed El-Kurd on Palestine and 'Perfect Victims,'" *Jezebel*, February 12, 2025, www.jezebel.com/on-trial-for-crimes-committed-against-you-mohammed-el-kurd-on-palestine-and-perfect-victims.

21 Mohammed El-Kurd, *Perfect Victims: And the Politics of Appeal* (Haymarket Books, 2025).

22 Mohammed El-Kurd, "'Do You Want to Throw Israelis into the Sea?'" *Nation*, July 1, 2025, www.thenation.com/article/world/mohammed-el-kurd -book-excerpt/.

23 Kylie Cheung, "'Israel Has a Right to Defend Itself' and the Language of Domestic Violence," *Prism*, December 11, 2023, https://prismreports.org /2023/12/11/israel-palestine-domestic-violence-darvo/.

24 Al Jazeera, "More than 100 Premature Babies in Gaza at Risk as Hospitals Run Out of Fuel," July 10, 2025, www.aljazeera.com/news/2025/7/10/more -than-100-premature-babies-at-risk-in-gaza-as-hospitals-run-out-of-fuel.

25 Reuters, "Biden Says He Has 'No Confidence' in Palestinian Death Count," October 25, 2023, www.reuters.com/world/middle-east/biden -says-he-has-no-confidence-palestinian-death-count-2023-10-26/.

26 CBS News, "Transcript: Florida Gov. Ron DeSantis on 'Face the Nation,'" October 15, 2023, www.cbsnews.com/news/ron-desantis-2024-hopeful -face-the-nation-transcript-01-07-2024/.

27 Blair Miller, "Zinke, Daines Introduce Bills Seeking to Block Palestinians from US," *Daily Montanan*, November 6, 2023, https://dailymontanan.com /2023/11/06/zinke-daines-introduce-bills-seeking-to-block-palestinians -from-us/.

28 Filip Timotija, "GOP Lawmaker Contends 'There Are Very Few Innocent Palestinian Citizens,'" *The Hill*, November 1, 2023, https://thehill.com /homenews/house/4288268-brian-mast-innocent-palestinian-civilians.

29 Akela Lacy, Prem Thakker, and Ryan Grim, "In Tense Closed-Door Meeting on Gaza, Josh Gottheimer Comment on Muslims Sparks Fury," *Intercept*, October 11, 2023, https://theintercept.com/2023/10/11/josh-gottheimer -muslims-jewish-imams.

30 Dana Bash, *State of the Union*, CNN, December 3, 2023, podcast, www.cnn .com/videos/politics/2023/12/03/sotu-jayapal-full-interview.cnn.

31 Sonam Sheth, "Netanyahu Deleted a Post on X About a Struggle Against 'Children of Darkness' Around the Time of a Tragic Hospital Explosion in Gaza," *Business Insider*, October 17, 2023, www.businessinsider.com /netanyahu-deleted-children-of-darkness-post-gaza-hospital-attack-2023-10.

CHAPTER 2

1 Mary Turfah, "Complicity: Seeing Everything but Palestinians," *Parapraxis*, July 13, 2025, www.cbsnews.com/news/ron-desantis-2024-hopeful-face -the-nation-transcript-01-07-2024/.

2 Ed Pilkington, "New York Mayoral Candidate Accuses Cuomo Donors of Altering Photo in Act of 'Blatant Islamophobia,'" *Guardian*, June 12, 2025, www.theguardian.com/us-news/2025/jun/12/nyc-mayoral-election -cuomo-mamdani-photo.

3 Mira Fox, "How Islamophobic Attacks on Zohran Mamdani Target Jewish Voters," *Forward*, June 25, 2025, https://forward.com/culture/732211/islamophobia-zohran-mamdani-nyc-mayor/.

4 Matthew Kassel, "Zohran Mamdani Says 'Globalize the Intifada' Is Expression of Palestinian Rights," *Jewish Insider*, June 17, 2025, https://jewishinsider.com/2025/06/zohran-mamdani-new-york-city-mayoral-israel-antisemitism/.

5 Jeff Coltin, "Gillibrand Apologizes to Mamdani Over 'Jihad' Comments," *Politico*, July 1, 2025, www.politico.com/news/2025/07/01/kirsten-gillibrand-zohran-mamdani-00436031.

6 Berl Falbaum, "New York Mayoral Vote Should Worry Jews Across the U.S.," Legal News, August 1, 2025, www.legalnews.com/Home/Articles?DataId=1586710.

7 Kylie Cheung, "'Israel Has a Right to Defend Itself' and the Language of Domestic Violence," *Prism*, December 11, 2023, https://prismreports.org/2023/12/11/israel-palestine-domestic-violence-darvo/.

8 CBS News, "New York Gov. Andrew Cuomo Jokes That Jews Have No Rhythm," March 26, 2018, www.cbsnews.com/news/new-york-gov-andrew-cuomo-jokes-that-jews-have-no-rhythm/.

9 Jeffery C. Mays, "Banned from YouTube, but Welcomed by Eric Adams at Gracie Mansion," *New York Times*, June 16, 2025, www.nytimes.com/2025/06/16/nyregion/adams-sneako-interview.html.

10 AlekseiTheBun, X.com, June 22, 2025, https://x.com/AlekseiTheBun/status/1936935883321770215.

11 Nick Reisman, "DOJ Says Andrew Cuomo Sexually Harassed 13 Women," *Politico*, January 26, 2024, www.politico.com/news/2024/01/26/cuomo-sexual-harassment-doj-00138140.

12 Adam Johnson, "Zohran Mamdani and the Anatomy of a Bogus 'Antisemitism' Scandal," *In These Times*, July 1, 2025, https://inthesetimes.com/article/zohran-mamdani-adl-antisemitism-intifada-bogus-scandal-nyc.

13 Mark Prussin, "NYPD Investigating Alleged Bomb Threat Against Zohran Mamdani," CBS News, June 19, 2025, www.cbsnews.com/newyork/news/zohran-mamdani-bomb-threat-investigation-nypd/.

14 Vanessa_ABee, X.com, June 28, 2025, https://x.com/Vanessa_ABee/status/1938916160533049795.

15 William A. Galston and Jordan Muchnick, "Support for Israel Continues to Deteriorate, Especially Among Democrats and Young People," Brookings, August 6, 2025, www.brookings.edu/articles/support-for-israel-continues-to-deteriorate-especially-among-democrats-and-young-people/.

16 *New York Times*, "Screams Without Words: How Hamas Weaponized Sexual Violence on Oct. 7," December 28, 2023, www.nytimes.com/2023/12/28/world/middleeast/oct-7-attacks-hamas-israel-sexual-violence.html.

17 *Mondoweiss*, "Family of Key Case in New York Times October 7 Sexual Violence Report Renounces Story, Says Reporters Manipulated Them," January 3, 2024, https://mondoweiss.net/2024/01/family-of-key-case-in-new-york-times-october-7-sexual-violence-report-renounces-story-says-reporters-manipulated-them/.
18 Ali Abunimah, "Watch: NY Times 'Investigation' of Mass Rape by Hamas Falls Apart," *Electronic Intifada*, January 9, 2024, https://electronicintifada.net/blogs/ali-abunimah/watch-ny-times-investigation-mass-rape-hamas-falls-apart.
19 Jeremy Scahill, Ryan Grim, and Daniel Boguslaw, "'Between the Hammer and the Anvil': The Story Behind the New York Times October 7 Exposé," *Intercept*, February 28, 2024, https://theintercept.com/2024/02/28/new-york-times-anat-schwartz-october-7/.
20 Kylie Cheung, "Palestinian Women Come Forward with Allegations of Increased Sexual Violence by Israeli Forces Since Oct. 7," *Prism*, March 4, 2025, https://prismreports.org/2025/03/04/palestinian-women-violence-israel-october-7/.
21 Jeremy Scahill, Ryan Grim, and Daniel Boguslaw, "'Between the Hammer and the Anvil': The Story Behind the New York Times October 7 Exposé," *Intercept*, February 28, 2024, https://theintercept.com/2024/02/28/new-york-times-anat-schwartz-october-7/.
22 *Times of Israel*, "'Where the Hell Are You?': Netanyahu Pans Rights Groups for Silence on Hamas Rape," December 5, 2023, www.timesofisrael.com/liveblog_entry/where-the-hell-are-you-netanyahu-pans-rights-groups-for-silence-on-hamas-rape/.
23 Liza Rozovsky, "Israel Blocks UN Probe into Hamas Sexual Crimes from October 7 to Avoid Inquiry into Abuse of Palestinians," *Haaretz*, January 8, 2025, www.haaretz.com/israel-news/2025-01-08/ty-article/.premium/israel-blocks-un-hamas-sexual-crimes-probe-to-avoid-inquiry-into-abuse-of-palestinians/00000194-44e0-d087-a9bd-7de1d5f20000.
24 Anna Krauthamer, "Grist of Empire," *Baffler*, February 11, 2025, https://thebaffler.com/latest/grist-of-empire-krauthamer.
25 Kylie Cheung, "Wartime Propaganda Experts Explain Why Israel's Social Media Strategy Is Targeting the West," *Prism*, November 29, 2023, https://prismreports.org/2023/11/29/why-israels-social-media-targeting-west/.
26 Miles Klee, "Israel's Social Media Chief Swears His Wild Campaign Is Working," *Rolling Stone*, November 10, 2023, www.rollingstone.com/culture/culture-features/israel-social-media-twitter-messaging-david-saranga-1234874381/.
27 Daniel Estrin, "Israel to Pay Students to Defend It Online," Associated Press, August 14, 2013, https://apnews.com/article/2b9d37b6d0ab4916bd5df9498ae4118f.

28 Ruth Marks Eglash, "Meet Israel's New Digital Diplomacy Chief," *Jewish Insider*, December 16, 2022, https://jewishinsider.com/2022/12/david-saranga-israel-digital-diplomacy-social-media-twitter/.

29 Data for Progress, "Voters Agree the U.S. Should Call for a Ceasefire and De-Escalation of Violence in Gaza to Prevent Civilian Deaths," October 20, 2023, www.dataforprogress.org/blog/2023/10/19/voters-agree-the-us-should-call-for-a-ceasefire-and-de-escalation-of-violence-in-gaza.

CHAPTER 3

1 Patrick Kingsley and Bilal Shbair, "Inside the Base Where Israel Has Detained Thousands of Gazans," *New York Times*, June 6, 2024, www.nytimes.com/2024/06/06/world/middleeast/israel-gaza-detention-base.html.

2 Al Jazeera, "Israeli Protesters Rally for 'the Right to Rape' Prisoners," August 13, 2024, www.aljazeera.com/video/newsfeed/2024/8/13/israeli-protesters-rally-for-the-right-to-rape-prisoners.

3 Al Jazeera, "Israeli Far-Right Politicians Protest Arrest of Soldiers Suspected of Abuse," July 29, 2024, www.aljazeera.com/news/2024/7/29/israeli-far-right-politicians-protest-arrest-of-soldiers-suspected-of-abuse.

4 Carnegie Endowment for International Peace, "Palestinian Prisoner Payments," 2023, https://carnegieendowment.org/features/palestinian-prisoner-payments?lang=en.

5 Mohamed A. Hussein and Mohammed Haddad, "A Nation Behind Bars: Why Has Israel Imprisoned 10,000 Palestinians?" Al Jazeera, April 17, 2025, www.aljazeera.com/news/2025/4/17/a-nation-behind-bars-why-has-israel-imprisoned-10000-palestinians.

6 Defense for Children–Palestine, "Military Detention," 2025, www.dci-palestine.org/tags/military_detention.

7 Wafa Ali Al-Udaini, "The Untold Stories of Palestinian Women Behind the Walls of Israeli Prisons," *Jezebel*, June 14, 2022, www.jezebel.com/palestinian-women-israeli-prisons-conditions-1849053677.

8 Kylie Cheung, "Israeli Airstrike Kills Palestinian Journalist Wafa Aludaini Alongside Her Entire Family," *Jezebel*, October 1, 2024, www.jezebel.com/israeli-airstrike-kills-palestinian-journalist-wafa-aludaini-her-entire-family.

9 Anna Krauthamer, "Grist of Empire," *Baffler*, February 11, 2025, https://thebaffler.com/latest/grist-of-empire-krauthamer.

10 Angela Y. Davis, Gina Dent, Erica R. Meiners, and Beth E. Richie, *Abolition. Feminism. Now.* (Haymarket Books, 2022).

11 Rana M. Jaleel, *The Work of Rape* (Duke University Press, 2021).

12 Ali Abunimah, "Israel Still Can't Find Any 7 October Rape Victims, Prosecutor Admits," *Electronic Intifada*, January 6, 2025, https://electronicintifada.net/blogs/ali-abunimah/israel-still-cant-find-any-7-october-rape-victims-prosecutor-admits.

13 Emanuel Fabian, "Defense Minister Announces 'Complete Siege' of Gaza: No Power, Food or Fuel," *Times of Israel*, October 9, 2023, www.timesofisrael .com/liveblog_entry/defense-minister-announces-complete-siege-of-gaza -no-power-food-or-fuel/.

14 NAACP, "History of Lynching in America," https://naacp.org/find-resources /history-explained/history-lynching-america.

15 Kylie Cheung, "Health Care Workers Say Conditions for Pregnant People in Gaza Are Getting Worse," *Jezebel*, August 30, 2024, www.jezebel.com /health-care-workers-say-conditions-for-pregnant-people-in-gaza-are -getting-worse.

16 Dania Akkad, "Israeli Soldiers Have Been Sexually Assaulting Palestinian Women for Decades. Now They're Speaking Out," *Middle East Eye*, December 3, 2024, www.middleeasteye.net/news/israel-sexual-assault -palestinian-women.

17 Jonathan Ofir, "The Main Suspect in the Sde Teiman Gang Rape Case Is Now a Media Star in Israel," *Mondoweiss*, August 28, 2024, https:// mondoweiss.net/2024/08/the-main-suspect-in-the-sde-teiman-gang-rape -case-is-now-a-media-star-in-israel/.

18 Anna Krauthamer, "Grist of Empire," *Baffler*, February 11, 2025, https:// thebaffler.com/latest/grist-of-empire-krauthamer.

19 Brett Murphy, "A Year of Empty Threats and a 'Smokescreen' Policy: How the State Department Let Israel Get Away with Horrors in Gaza," *ProPublica*, January 15, 2025, www.propublica.org/article/biden-blinken-state -department-israel-gaza-human-rights-horrors.

20 Danny, "Israel: 240 Palestinian Children 'Sexually Abused' in Jerusalem Detention Centres, Group Claims," Middle East Children's Alliance, December 2, 2014, www.mecaforpeace.org/israel-240-palestinian-children -sexually-abused-in-jerusalem-detention-centres-group-claims/.

21 UN Independent International Commission of Inquiry on the Occupied Palestinian Territory, Including East Jerusalem, and Israel, "'More than a Human Can Bear': Israel's Systematic Use of Sexual, Reproductive and Other Forms of Gender-Based Violence Since October 2023," March 13, 2025, www.un.org/unispal/document/report-of-commisison-of-inquiry -opt-13march2025/.

22 Kylie Cheung, "In Gaza, the Gender-Based Violence Against Palestinians 'Can Only Be Described as Systematic,'" *Jezebel*, March 24, 2025, www .jezebel.com/in-gaza-the-gender-based-violence-against-palestinians-can -only-be-described-as-systematic.

23 United Nations Human Rights, "'More than a Human Can Bear': Israel's Systematic Use of Sexual, Reproductive and Other Forms of Gender-Based Violence Since October 2023," press release, March 13, 2025, www.ohchr.org /en/press-releases/2025/03/more-human-can-bear-israels-systematic-use -sexual-reproductive-and-other.

CHAPTER 4

1 Mahmoud Khalil, "To My Newborn Son: I Am Absent Not Out of Apathy, but Conviction," *Guardian*, May 11, 2025, www.theguardian.com/commentisfree/2025/may/10/mahmoud-kahlil-letter-to-newborn-son.

2 Al Jazeera, "Gaza Faces 'Largest Orphan Crisis' in Modern History, Report Says," April 3, 2025, www.aljazeera.com/news/2025/4/3/gaza-faces-largest-orphan-crisis-in-modern-history-report-says.

3 Nedal Samir Hamdouna, Aseel Mousa, and Julian Borger, "The Plight of Gaza's 'WCNSFs'—Wounded Child, No Surviving Family," *Guardian*, December 22, 2023, www.theguardian.com/world/2023/dec/22/the-plight-of-gazas-wcnsfs-wounded-child-no-surviving-family.

4 UNRWA, "UNRWA Situation Report #87 on the Situation in the Gaza Strip and the West Bank, Including East Jerusalem," March 8, 2024, www.unrwa.org/resources/reports/unrwa-situation-report-87-situation-gaza-strip-and-west-bank-including-east-Jerusalem.

5 ARC-Southeast, "Letter: Reproductive Justice Includes Palestinian Liberation," October 24, 2023, https://arc-southeast.org/2023/10/24/rj-includes-palestine/.

6 Ja'Loni Amor Owens, "Mahmoud Khalil's Detainment Is a Reproductive Justice Issue," *Prism*, March 13, 2025, https://prismreports.org/2025/03/13/mahmoud-khalil-reproductive-justice/.

7 M. G. E. Kelly, *Biopolitical Imperialism* (Collective Ink, 2015).

8 Kylie Cheung, "Your State Probably Still Allows Forced Sterilizations," *Jezebel*, January 26, 2022, www.jezebel.com/your-state-probably-still-allows-forced-sterilizations-1848425014.

9 Kylie Cheung, "Miscarriages in Gaza Have Increased 300% Under Israeli Bombing," *Jezebel*, January 17, 2024, www.jezebel.com/miscarriages-in-gaza-have-increased-300-under-israeli-1851168680.

10 Kylie Cheung, "Health Care Workers Say Conditions for Pregnant People in Gaza Are Getting Worse," *Jezebel*, August 30, 2024, www.jezebel.com/health-care-workers-say-conditions-for-pregnant-people-in-gaza-are-getting-worse.

11 Kylie Cheung, "Inside Gaza's Primary Maternity Hospital Where Babies Are Being Born Smaller, Premature, and with Congenital Disorders," *Jezebel*, April 10, 2024, www.jezebel.com/inside-gazas-primary-maternity-hospital-where-babies-are-being-born-smaller-premature-and-with-congenital-disorders.

12 Samah Shamali, Facebook, January 26, 2024, www.facebook.com/samah.shamali.5/posts/pfbid02t21vRjgGsDfyjaQAiBnQX5EnSLbFj7Yw22FgDiwVeWnK6F6U9ftWRf321BiK1cddl.

13 Kylie Cheung, "Reproductive Health Crises in Gaza Will Only Worsen as U.S. Withdraws UNRWA Funding," *Jezebel*, February 15, 2024,

www.jezebel.com/reproductive-health-crises-in-gaza-will-only-worsen-as-u-s-withdraws-unrwa-funding.

14 Ammal Awadallah, Instagram, July 9, 2024, www.instagram.com/p/C9Ma-LVufuw/?hl=en&img_index=7.

15 Bilal Irfan, Abdallah Abu Shammala, and Khaled Saleh, "Will There Be a Future for Newborns in Gaza?" *Lancet* 404, no. 10464 (November 2, 2024): 1725–1726, https://doi.org/10.1016/S0140-6736(24)02249-9.

16 Kylie Cheung, "U.S. Doctors Back from Gaza Say the DNC Speeches, Rhetoric Feel Like an Alternate Reality," *Jezebel*, August 20, 2024, www.jezebel.com/american-doctors-back-from-gaza-say-the-dnc-speeches-rhetoric-feel-like-an-alternate-reality.

17 USA Letter, Gaza Healthcare Letters, October 2, 2024, www.gazahealthcareletters.org/usa-letter-oct-2-2024.

18 UN Independent International Commission of Inquiry on the Occupied Palestinian Territory, Including East Jerusalem, and Israel, "'More than a Human Can Bear': Israel's Systematic Use of Sexual, Reproductive and Other Forms of Gender-Based Violence Since October 2023," March 13, 2025, www.un.org/unispal/document/report-of-commisison-of-inquiry-opt-13march2025/.

19 Kylie Cheung, "So, the Internet Is Swooning Over the Suspected UnitedHealthcare Assassin," *Jezebel*, December 6, 2024, www.jezebel.com/so-the-internet-is-swooning-over-the-unitedhealthcare-assassin.

20 David Armstrong, Patrick Rucker, and Maya Miller, "UnitedHealthcare Tried to Deny Coverage to a Chronically Ill Patient. He Fought Back, Exposing the Insurer's Inner Workings," *ProPublica*, February 2, 2023, www.propublica.org/article/unitedhealth-healthcare-insurance-denial-ulcerative-colitis.

21 Casey Ross and Bob Herman, "UnitedHealth Pushed Employees to Follow an Algorithm to Cut Off Medicare Patients' Rehab Care," STAT News, November 14, 2023, www.statnews.com/2023/11/14/unitedhealth-algorithm-medicare-advantage-investigation/.

22 David Cohen, "Vitriol Following Insurance Executive's Slaying Not a Surprise, Ro Khanna Says," *Politico*, December 8, 2024, www.politico.com/news/2024/12/08/ceo-slain-ro-khanna-00193188.

23 Lauren Sforza, "Blunt Democratic Senator Roasts Those Cheering CEO's Killing," NJ.com, December 17, 2024, www.nj.com/politics/2024/12/blunt-democratic-senator-roasts-those-cheering-ceos-killing.html.

24 Kylie Cheung, "The Supreme Court Wants Privacy? So Do We," *Jezebel*, May 9, 2022, www.jezebel.com/the-supreme-court-wants-privacy-so-do-we-1848900007.

25 Andrew P. Wilper, Steffie Woolhandler, Karen E. Lasser, Danny McCormick, David H. Bor, and David U. Himmelstein, "Health Insurance and Mortality

in US Adults," *American Journal of Public Health* 99, no. 12 (December 2009): 2289–2295, https://doi.org/10.2105/AJPH.2008.157685.

26 American Bankruptcy Institute, "Over 60% of Bankruptcies Caused by Medical Bills," www.abi.org/feed-item/over-60-of-bankruptcies-caused-by-medical-bills.

27 Juliann Ventura, "Warren: 'Visceral' Response to Insurance CEO's Killing Should Be 'Warning to Everyone in the Health Care System,'" *The Hill*, December 11, 2024, https://thehill.com/policy/healthcare/5034574-elizabeth-warren-unitedhealthcare-ceo-shooting-response-warning/.

28 Denise Chow, Tavleen Tarrant, and Patrick Martin, "On Reddit Account Linked to Luigi Mangione, Posts Describe Back Pain and Spinal Surgery," NBC News, December 11, 2024, www.nbcnews.com/news/us-news/reddit-account-linked-luigi-mangione-back-pain-surgery-rcna183674.

29 Kylie Cheung, "Daniel Penny, Who Strangled Jordan Neely for 6 Minutes, Found Not Guilty of Strangling Him to Death," *Jezebel*, December 9, 2024, www.jezebel.com/daniel-penny-acquittal.

30 Akela Lacy, "How to Not Get Arrested After Killing Someone in Public," *Intercept*, May 3, 2023, https://theintercept.com/2023/05/03/nypd-jordan-neely-strangled-subway/.

31 Julia Mueller, "Online Fund Raises Nearly $2 Million for Daniel Penny's Legal Defense in Subway Case," *The Hill*, May 14, 2023, https://thehill.com/blogs/blog-briefing-room/4004207-online-fund-raises-nearly-2-million-for-daniel-pennys-legal-defense-in-subway-case/.

32 ABC News, "Cops Bought Burger King for Dylann Roof Following His Arrest," June 23, 2015, https://abc7.com/post/cops-bought-burger-king-for-dylann-roof-following-his-arrest/801013/.

33 Kylie Cheung, "Eric Adams & the NYPD Held a Theatrical Photo Shoot with Luigi Mangione," *Jezebel*, December 20, 2024, www.jezebel.com/eric-adams-nypd-luigi-mangione-perp-walk.

34 Leah Sarnoff, "Florida Woman Charged for Threatening Health Insurance Company: 'Delay, Deny, Depose,'" ABC News, December 12, 2024, https://abcnews.go.com/US/florida-woman-charged-threatening-health-insurance-company-delay/story?id=116748222.

CHAPTER 5

1 Kylie Cheung, "Judge Dismisses Murder Charge Against Tracy McCarter, Who Stabbed Her Violent Ex in Self-Defense," *Jezebel*, December 5, 2022, www.jezebel.com/judge-dismisses-murder-charge-against-tracy-mccarter-w-1849853705.

2 Kylie Cheung, "Joe Biden Should Grant Clemency to Criminalized Survivors," *Jezebel*, December 20, 2024, www.jezebel.com/joe-biden-should-grant-clemency-to-criminalized-survivors-but-we-cant-stop-there.

3 Kylie Cheung, "Trial Begins for Ray Garcia, Warden of Prison Nicknamed the 'Rape Club,'" *Jezebel*, November 30, 2022, www.jezebel.com/trial-begins-for-ray-garcia-warden-of-prison-nicknamed-1849836112.

4 Sam Levin, "Survivors of Prison Sexual Abuse Scandal Ask Biden for Clemency: 'Give Us a Chance,'" *Guardian*, December 18, 2024, www.theguardian.com/us-news/ng-interactive/2024/dec/18/prison-sexual-abuse-survivors-biden-clemency.

5 US Senate Permanent Subcommittee on Investigations, "Sexual Abuse of Female Inmates in Federal Prisons: Staff Report," December 13, 2022, www.govinfo.gov/content/pkg/GOVPUB-Y4_G74_9-PURL-gpo189780/pdf/GOVPUB-Y4_G74_9-PURL-gpo189780.pdf.

6 Alisa Bierria and Colby Lenz, eds., "Defending Self-Defense: A Call to Action by Survived & Punished," Survived & Punished, March 2022, https://survivedandpunished.org/wp-content/uploads/2024/03/DSD-Report-Sep-2022.pdf.

7 Andrew Van Dam, "Less than 1% of Rapes Lead to Felony Convictions. At Least 89% of Victims Face Emotional and Physical Consequences," *Washington Post*, October 6, 2018, www.washingtonpost.com/business/2018/10/06/less-than-percent-rapes-lead-felony-convictions-least-percent-victims-face-emotional-physical-consequences/.

8 Battered Women's Justice Project, "The Intersection of Domestic Violence and Child Custody," October 8, 2024, https://bwjp.org/wp-content/uploads/2024/10/Childrens-Fact-Sheet-UPDATED.pdf.

9 Kylie Cheung, "Violence Deconstructed: Hysteria Over Zohran Mamdani's Crime Platform Is Rooted in Lie That Cops Make Women Safer," *Prism*, July 29, 2025, https://prismreports.org/2025/07/29/zohran-mamdani-police-domestic-violence/.

10 Leigh Goodmark, "Law Enforcement Experience Report," National Domestic Violence Hotline, 2022, www.niwrc.org/sites/default/files/DV%20and%20LE%20Collection/2209-Hotline-LES_FINAL.pdf.

11 RAINN, "Statistics: The Criminal Justice System," August 28, 2025, https://rainn.org/facts-statistics-the-scope-of-the-problem/statistics-the-criminal-justice-system/.

12 Cameron Kimble, "Sexual Assault Remains Dramatically Underreported," Brennan Center for Justice, October 4, 2018, www.brennancenter.org/our-work/analysis-opinion/sexual-assault-remains-dramatically-underreported.

13 Amia Srinivasan, *The Right to Sex* (Farrar, Straus and Giroux, 2021).

14 Kylie Cheung, "Officers Who Handled Gabby Petito Murder Case Should Be Placed on Probation, Says New Report," *Jezebel*, January 14, 2022, www.jezebel.com/officers-who-handled-gabby-petito-murder-case-should-be-1848361389.

15 Kylie Cheung, "Officer Who Pulled Over Gabby Petito Once Allegedly Threatened to Kill His Girlfriend," *Jezebel*, November 4, 2022, www.jezebel.com/officer-who-pulled-over-gabby-petito-once-allegedly-thr-1849743078.

16 Melissa Jeltsen, "Police Are Cutting Ties with Domestic Violence Programs That Support Black Lives Matter," *HuffPost*, October 21, 2020, www.huffpost.com/entry/domestic-violence-black-lives-matter-police_n_5f88c8a1c5b66ee9a5ee43d7.

17 Kylie Cheung, "How ICE Raids Are Making It Easier for Civilian Men to Assault Immigrant Women," *Teen Vogue*, September 22, 2025, www.teenvogue.com/story/men-dressed-as-ice-agents-to-assault-immigrant-women-horrifying-trend.

18 Angela Y. Davis, Gina Dent, Erica R. Meiners, and Beth E. Richie, *Abolition. Feminism. Now.* (Haymarket Books, 2022).

19 Sarah Nesbitt and Sage Carson, "The Cost of Reporting: Perpetrator Retaliation, Institutional Betrayal, and Student Survivor Pushout," Advocates for Youth, 2021, www.advocatesforyouth.org/wp-content/uploads/2024/06/Know-Your-IX-2021-Cost-of-Reporting.pdf.

20 Kylie Cheung, "Men Accused of Sexual Misconduct on Campuses Are Suing Over 'Anti-Male Bias,' and It's Working," *Jezebel*, January 13, 2022, www.jezebel.com/men-accused-of-sexual-misconduct-on-campuses-are-suing-1848347194.

21 Kylie Cheung, "California Bill Aims to Protect Sexual Assault Survivors from Getting Sued by Their Assailants," *Jezebel*, September 28, 2023, www.jezebel.com/california-bill-aims-to-protect-sexual-assault-survivor-1850878333.

22 California State Legislature, California Assembly Bill 933, LegiScan, October 10, 2023, https://legiscan.com/CA/text/AB933/id/2845352.

23 Sarah DeGue, "The Cost of Rape," National Sexual Violence Resource Center, December 4, 2018, https://nsvrc.org/blog_post/cost-rape/.

24 Kylie Cheung, "Sexual Assault Survivors Are Being Billed Thousands for Emergency Care," *Jezebel*, September 14, 2022, www.jezebel.com/sexual-assault-survivors-are-being-billed-thousands-for-1849534311.

25 Kylie Cheung, "There Have Been Tens of Thousands of Rape-Induced Pregnancies Post-*Roe*," *Jezebel*, February 2, 2024, www.jezebel.com/rape-induced-pregnancy-roe-dobbs-abortion-ban-1851209068.

26 David Remnick, "The Custody Battles Awaiting Mothers of Children Conceived in Rape," New Yorker Radio Hour, January 31, 2023, podcast, www.wnycstudios.org/podcasts/tnyradiohour/articles/custody-battles-awaiting-mothers-children-conceived-rape.

27 Olivia Reingold, "NYPD Cops: 'I Will Quit if Zohran Is Elected,'" *Free Press*, October 7, 2025, www.thefp.com/p/nypd-cops-i-will-quit-if-zohran-is-mayor.

28 Ernesto Lopez and Bobby Boxerman, "Crime Trends in U.S. Cities: Mid-Year 2025 Update," Council on Criminal Justice, July 11, 2025, https://counciloncj.org/crime-trends-in-u-s-cities-mid-year-2025-update/.
29 Everytown, "Gun Violence by Police," May 27, 2025, www.everytown.org/issues/gun-violence-by-police/.
30 Dave McKenna, X.com, June 7, 2020, https://x.com/djmckenna00/status/1269579021148446721.

CHAPTER 6

1 Kylie Cheung, "All-Male Anti-Abortion Panel Calls for Death Penalty," *Jezebel*, July 25, 2023, www.jezebel.com/all-male-anti-abortion-panel-calls-for-death-penalty-1850674781.
2 Kavitha Surana, Mariam Elba, Cassandra Jaramillo, Robin Fields, and Ziva Branstetter, "Are Abortion Bans Across America Causing Deaths? The States That Passed Them Are Doing Little to Find Out," *ProPublica*, December 18, 2024, www.propublica.org/article/abortion-bans-deaths-state-maternal-mortality-committees.
3 Kylie Cheung, "We're Now Up to 10 States Trying to Charge Abortion Patients with Homicide," *Jezebel*, March 31, 2025, www.jezebel.com/were-now-up-to-10-states-trying-to-charge-abortion-patients-with-homicide.
4 Purvaja S. Kavattur et al., "The Rise of Pregnancy Criminalization," Pregnancy Justice, September 2023, https://search.issuelab.org/resource/the-rise-of-pregnancy-criminalization-a-pregnancy-justice-report.html.
5 Pregnancy Justice, "Pregnancy Justice Launches Pregnancy Is Not a Crime Campaign, Calls for Healthcare Not Handcuffs," press release, November 12, 2025, www.pregnancyjusticeus.org/press/pregnancy-justice-launches-pregnancy-is-not-a-crime-campaign.
6 Pregnancy Justice, "Pregnancy as a Crime: An Interim Update on the First Two Years After Dobbs," September 30, 2025, www.pregnancyjusticeus.org/wp-content/uploads/2025/09/Pregnancy-as-a-Crime-An-Interim-Update-on-the-First-Two-Years-After-Dobbs.pdf.
7 National Domestic Violence Hotline, "Reproductive Coercion and Abuse Report," June 2024, www.thehotline.org/wp-content/uploads/media/2024/06/reproductive-coercion-and-abuse-report-final.pdf.
8 Center for Reproductive Rights, "President Trump Pardons 23 People Who Harassed and Attacked Abortion Patients and Clinics," press release, January 24, 2025, https://reproductiverights.org/news/trump-pardons-23-people-attacked-abortion-patients-clinics/.
9 Kylie Cheung, "Trump Effectively Greenlights Anti-Abortion Violence," *Jezebel*, January 27, 2025, www.jezebel.com/trump-effectively-greenlights-anti-abortion-violence.

10 Linnaea Honl-Stuenkel, "At Least 10 Pardoned Insurrectionists Face Other Criminal Charges," Citizens for Responsibility and Ethics in Washington, June 4, 2025, www.citizensforethics.org/reports-investigations/crew-investigations/at-least-10-pardoned-insurrectionists-face-other-criminal-charges/.

11 National Abortion Federation, "NAF 2024 Violence & Disruption Report," 2025, https://prochoice.org/our-work/provider-security/2024-naf-violence-disruption/.

12 KRDO News, "Self-Proclaimed Planned Parenthood Gunman Calls Shooting 'Righteous Crusade,'" February 29, 2016, https://krdo.com/news/2016/02/29/self-proclaimed-planned-parenthood-gunman-calls-shooting-righteous-crusade/.

13 Trans Legislation Tracker, "What Anti-Trans Bills Passed in 2025?" 2025, https://translegislation.com/bills/2025/passed.

14 Orion Rummier, "House Republicans Advance Sweeping Anti-Trans Bills Ahead of Holiday Break," The 19th, December 17, 2025, https://19thnews.org/2025/12/congress-trans-health-care-ban/.

15 Asma Khalid, "Harris Tries to Flip the Script on Trump on the Border During Raucous Georgia Speech," NPR, July 30, 2024, www.wesa.fm/2024-07-30/harris-tries-to-flip-the-script-on-trump-on-the-border-during-raucous-georgia-speech.

16 Kylie Cheung, "Survivor Advocates Say the Anti-Immigrant Laken Riley Act Is Exploiting Their Cause," *Jezebel*, January 14, 2025, www.jezebel.com/survivor-advocates-say-the-anti-immigrant-laken-riley-act-is-exploiting-their-cause.

17 Kylie Cheung, "Survivor Advocates Say the Anti-Immigrant Laken Riley Act Is Exploiting Their Cause."

18 Kylie Cheung, "Attention-Seeking Bigot Claims Immigrants Are 'Raping Our Women' to Justify Bill That Could Harm Survivors," *Jezebel*, January 30, 2025, www.jezebel.com/attention-seeking-bigot-claims-immigrants-are-raping-our-women-to-justify-bill-that-could-harm-survivors.

19 Kylie Cheung, "Attention-Seeking Bigot Claims Immigrants Are 'Raping Our Women' to Justify Bill That Could Harm Survivors."

20 Jessica Washington, "Republicans Say This Anti-Immigrant Bill Will Protect Victims of Abuse. It Will Do the Opposite," *Intercept*, January 24, 2025, https://theintercept.com/2025/01/24/republicans-violence-women-deport-immigrants/.

21 World Health Organization, "Violence Against Women," March 25, 2024, www.who.int/news-room/fact-sheets/detail/violence-against-women.

22 Everytown, "Guns and Violence Against Women," May 27, 2025, https://everytownresearch.org/report/guns-and-violence-against-women/.

23 Kylie Cheung, "Risk of Maternal Mortality Is Twice as High in Abortion-Banned States, New Study Says," *Jezebel*, April 23, 2025, www.jezebel.com/risk-of-maternal-mortality-is-twice-as-high-in-abortion-banned-states-new-study-says.

24 National Task Force to End Sexual and Domestic Violence, "Letter in Opposition to HR 30," January 13, 2025, www.4vawa.org/ntf-action-alerts-and-news/2025/1/13/letter-in-opposition-to-hr-30-1.

25 Jessica Washington, "This Small Change May Save Domestic Violence Survivors from Partners Who Abuse the Child Welfare System," *Jezebel*, June 5, 2024, www.jezebel.com/this-small-change-may-save-domestic-violence-survivors-from-partners-who-abuse-the-child-welfare-system.

26 Jessica Washington, "Republicans Say This Anti-Immigrant Bill Will Protect Victims of Abuse. It Will Do the Opposite," *Intercept*, January 24, 2025, https://theintercept.com/2025/01/24/republicans-violence-women-deport-immigrants/.

27 Hannah Greene, "The State of Missouri Lynched Marcellus 'Khaliifah' Williams," *Prism*, October 17, 2024, https://prismreports.org/2024/10/17/the-state-of-missouri-lynched-marcellus-khaliifah-williams/.

28 Kylie Cheung, "Looks Like Greg Abbott Failed to 'Eliminate Rape,'" *Jezebel*, December 23, 2024, www.jezebel.com/greg-abbott-pledged-to-eliminate-rape-now-hes-warning-those-who-cross-border-will-be-raped.

29 CBS News, "Border Patrol Official: Young Girls Illegally Entering US Given Birth Control, Plan B," June 19, 2018, www.cbsnews.com/losangeles/news/border-patrol-immigration-plan-b-birth-control/.

30 Alice Speri, "Detained, Then Violated," *Intercept*, April 11, 2018, https://justdetention.org/detained-then-violated/.

31 Ariel G. Ruiz Soto, "Explainer: Immigrants and Crime in the United States," Migration Policy Institute, October 2024, www.migrationpolicy.org/content/immigrants-and-crime.

32 Luke Garrett, "Vance Defends Spreading Claims That Haitian Migrants Are Eating Pets," NPR, September 15, 2024, www.npr.org/2024/09/15/nx-s1-5113140/vance-false-claims-haitian-migrants-pets.

33 American Immigration Council, "What's in the Big Beautiful Bill? Immigration and Border Security Unpacked," July 14, 2025, www.americanimmigrationcouncil.org/fact-sheet/big-beautiful-bill-immigration-border-security/.

34 Kylie Cheung, "How ICE Raids Are Making It Easier for Civilian Men to Assault Immigrant Women," *Teen Vogue*, September 22, 2025, www.teenvogue.com/story/men-dressed-as-ice-agents-to-assault-immigrant-women-horrifying-trend.

35 Susanna Capelouto, "Whistleblower in Georgia Claims High Number of Hysterectomies at ICE Facility," NPR, September 16, 2020, www.npr.org

/2020/09/16/913448209/whistleblower-in-georgia-claims-high-number-of-hysterectomies-at-ice-facility.

36 US House Democratic Women's Caucus, letter to DHS, August 11, 2025, https://juliabrownley.house.gov/wp-content/uploads/2025/08/dwc-letter-to-dhs-on-ice-impersonators-and-women-s-safety.pdf.

37 Kylie Cheung, "Police Officers Can't Rape People and Claim There Was 'Consent' Anymore," *Jezebel*, March 17, 2022, www.jezebel.com/police-officers-cant-rape-people-and-claim-there-was-co-1848667095.

CHAPTER 7

1 Lanre Bakare, "Angela Davis: 'We Knew That the Role of the Police Was to Protect White Supremacy,'" *Guardian*, June 15, 2020, www.theguardian.com/us-news/2020/jun/15/angela-davis-on-george-floyd-as-long-as-the-violence-of-racism-remains-no-one-is-safe.

2 Angela Davis, *Freedom Is a Constant Struggle* (Haymarket Books, 2016).

3 Communist Party USA, "Mass Protest, Not Individual Acts of Violence, Builds Social Change," July 15, 2024, www.cpusa.org/article/engaging-millions-in-mass-protest-not-violence-is-the-path-to-social-change/.

4 Jackie Wang, *Carceral Capitalism* (Semiotext(e), 2018).

5 David Ingram, "Trump Turns the White House Lawn into a Tesla Showroom," NBC News, March 11, 2025, www.nbcnews.com/tech/elon-musk/trump-musk-tesla-white-house-showroom-buys-car-rcna195905.

6 Che Guevara, *Guerrilla Warfare: A Method*, Marxists Internet Archive, September 1963, www.marxists.org/archive/guevara/1963/09/guerrilla-warfare.htm.

7 Ernesto "Che" Guevara, *Guerrilla Warfare* (1961).

8 Richard Carleton interview of Ghassan Kanafani, YouTube, Beirut, October 16, 1970, www.youtube.com/watch?v=pRXPImNyMXM.

9 Jewish Voice for Peace, Instagram, 2023, www.instagram.com/reels/CzD8hAJSXUx/.

10 Danny Rubinstein, *Why Didn't You Bang on the Sides of the Tank?* (Yedioth Books, 2022).

11 Dylan Saba, X.com, August 1, 2025, https://x.com/shaabiranks/status/1951278241118851123.

12 Leon Trotsky, "Why Marxists Oppose Individual Terrorism," November 1911, www.marxists.org/archive/trotsky/1911/11/tia09.htm.

13 Peter Camejo, "Liberalism, Ultraleftism or Mass Action," June 14, 1970, www.marxists.org/archive/camejo/1970/ultraleftismormassaction.htm.

14 Lex Von Klark, "What Is Ultraleftism?" Young Democratic Socialists of America, March 2, 2021, https://y.dsausa.org/the-activist/what-is-ultraleftism/.

15 Gareth Watkins, "AI: The New Aesthetics of Fascism," *New Socialist*, February 9, 2025, https://newsocialist.org.uk/transmissions/ai-the-new-aesthetics-of-fascism/.

CHAPTER 8

1 Anna North, "'Your Body, My Choice': The Misogynist MAGA Attack, Explained," *Vox*, November 13, 2024, www.vox.com/politics/384792/your-body-my-choice-maga-gender-election.

2 Trevor Project, "The Trevor Project Reports 200% Increase in Election Conversations Across Its Crisis Services," November 5, 2024, www.thetrevorproject.org/blog/media-alert-the-trevor-project-reports-200-increase-in-election-conversations-across-its-crisis-services/.

3 Kylie Cheung, "Searches for Birth Control, Abortion Pills Are Spiking. Here's What You Need to Know," *Jezebel*, November 8, 2024, www.jezebel.com/searches-for-birth-control-abortion-pills-are-spiking-heres-what-you-need-to-know.

4 Kylie Cheung, "Inside the Network of Manosphere Influencers Who Have Pushed Young Men to the Right," *Jezebel*, November 18, 2024, www.jezebel.com/inside-the-network-of-manosphere-influencers-who-have-pushed-young-men-to-the-right.

5 Kylie Cheung, "Report Finds Evidence of Widespread, Anti-Amber Heard Online Harassment Campaign," *Jezebel*, July 18, 2022, www.jezebel.com/report-finds-evidence-of-widespread-anti-amber-heard-o-1849190429.

6 Reid J. Epstein, Lisa Lerer, and Nicholas Nehamas, "Devastated Democrats Play the Blame Game, and Stare at a Dark Future," *New York Times*, November 11, 2024, www.nytimes.com/2024/11/07/us/politics/democrats-kamala-harris.html.

7 National Abortion Federation, "NAF 2024 Violence & Disruption Report," 2025, https://prochoice.org/our-work/provider-security/2024-naf-violence-disruption/.

8 Audra Heinrichs, "A Data Firm Was Tracking People Who Visited Abortion Clinics and Selling the Data," *Jezebel*, May 3, 2022, www.jezebel.com/a-data-firm-is-tracking-people-who-visit-abortion-clini-1848875722.

9 Guttmacher Institute, "Abortion Reporting Requirements," December 1, 2025, www.guttmacher.org/state-policy/explore/abortion-reporting-requirements.

10 Susan Rinkunas, "This State Could Police Your Sex Positions if *Roe v. Wade* Is Overturned," *Jezebel*, March 18, 2022, www.jezebel.com/this-state-could-police-your-sex-positions-if-roe-v-wa-1848672011.

11 Matthew Olay, "Senior Officials Outline President's Proposed FY26 Defense Budget," US Department of War, June 26, 2025, www.war.gov/News/News-Stories/Article/article/4227847/senior-officials-outline-presidents-proposed-fy26-defense-budget/.

12 Ernesto "Che" Guevara, *Guerrilla Warfare* (1961).

INDEX

I

J

K

L

M

N

O

P

R

ABOUT THE AUTHOR

Photo © by Melina Mae Castorillo

Kylie Cheung is a journalist and the author of four other books on gender and politics, including *Survivor Injustice: State-Sanctioned Abuse, Domestic Violence, and the Fight for Bodily Autonomy*, which *Kirkus* called "an astonishingly original, powerfully honest vision for true survivor justice," and *Coercion: Surviving and Resisting Abortion Bans*. She is based in Brooklyn.

ABOUT NORTH ATLANTIC BOOKS

North Atlantic Books (NAB) is an independent, nonprofit publisher committed to a bold exploration of the relationships between mind, body, spirit, and nature. Founded in 1974, NAB aims to nurture a holistic view of the arts, sciences, humanities, and healing. To make a donation or to learn more about our books, authors, events, and newsletter, please visit www.northatlanticbooks.com.